# DIVORCE
legal procedures
and financial facts

a Consumer Publication

Consumers' Association
publishers of **Which?**
2 Marylebone Road
London NW1 4DX

a Consumer Publication

*edited by*   Edith Rudinger

*published by*   Consumers' Association
publishers of **Which?**

Which? Books are commissioned and researched by The Association for Consumer Research
and published by Consumers' Association, 2 Marylebone Road, London NW1 4DX and
Hodder and Stoughton, 47 Bedford Square, London WC1B 3DP

ISBN 0 340 393 475
and   0 85202 343 47X

Photoset by Paston Press, Loddon, Norfolk
Printed by Hazell Watson & Viney Limited.

# CONTENTS

# DIVORCE AND YOUR POCKET

Divorce has become relatively easy to obtain, but many people still see the divorce decree as the main hurdle. It is not – the major problems are nearly always about money, housing and children. If and when divorce comes, you may not expect it to be the financial disaster that it can turn out to be.

You may have to cope with many intense emotions: perhaps a sense of failure, loneliness and depression, feelings of resentment or hatred towards your partner and distress over the children. Alternatively, you may find yourself on a temporary 'high' from feelings of release and the prospect of a new beginning. While all this is going on, it may not be easy to think sensibly about financial arrangements, apart from the short-term provision of everyday needs for yourself and your children – getting through the next day is often as much as you can cope with.

It may be months or even years before your emotions settle down, indeed they may never do so, but one thing is certain – your life and the way you live is bound to change.

### spending rush
Faced with a broken marriage, it is not uncommon for life to seem unreal and one of the ways in which this sometimes comes out is a surge in your impulse spending – assuming the money is there (and often even if it is not).

You may find yourself wanting to blow money on redecorating or re-equipping the house. You may go out more often to avoid being alone or to try and start new relationships. If you sit it out at home, staying up until the early hours of the morning talking on the telephone to friends, you may find that the heating and lighting and 'phone bills go up; you may start spending more money on cigarettes and alcohol.

*standard of living*

Whatever your standard of living was before the divorce, you have to accept that it is going to drop, often quite drastically, especially where you have children and/or only one of you is working. Be realistic: do not expect that somehow there will be more money than there was before.

In some cases, money is so limited that it would be quite pointless arguing for months, either privately or with the assistance of solicitors: unless the money facts change, there is nothing that can be done. The problem nearly always comes down to the fact that two homes have to be found and run, rather than one. The sooner you come to terms with this, the better for everybody.

Although you and your partner are divorcing because the marriage relationship between the two of you has come to an end, you should still be able to trust each other as rational intelligent people – at least enough to make proper arrangements for your children's future and your own.

Like it or not, realities have to be faced and the sooner you and your husband or wife get down to sorting out your financial affairs the better.

**ways in which divorce will hit your pocket**

Not all of the ways in which people suffer financially on divorce will apply to your situation. For example, if you are both in your late twenties, have no children and both have good jobs and have been buying a house together on mortgage for the last few years, it may be that you can split up without it costing either of you too much. On the other hand, if you have small children, or one of you is unemployed, or has not worked for many years, you are both going to suffer, because there will now be two households and only one income to support them.

*two homes to run and furnish*

As well as the rent or mortgage and the bills for rates, water charges, gas and electricity to be paid on the matrimonial home, money for similar charges will now have to be found for a new home by or for the person who is moving out.

Generally, whoever is moving out will suffer, at least temporarily, a substantial reduction in the quality of his or her home environment.

Quite apart from the running costs, even if you agree to split the contents of your existing home, there may still be the cost of buying some duplicate furniture and items of household equipment – another cooker, refrigerator and possibly a washing machine – unless one of you is moving into an already furnished flat, or lodgings.

The person who remains may well find that he or she does not have sufficient money to run the house in the same way as before. The wife may not be fully aware of the cost of heating and lighting the house and may be completely unprepared for the bills when they start to come in.

If you are the spouse left behind in the home, you should not assume that you will be able to afford to stay there, even if you can get maintenance or some other financial support. One side-effect of the break-up of the marriage may be that you lose your job or have to give it up and then cannot continue to make the mortgage payments.

*costs of moving*

If whoever is moving out is buying a home, there may be some or all of

- conveyancing fees
- solicitors' fees connected with mortgage
- surveyors' fees
- mortgage broker's fee (you may need help to find a mortgage on a second home)
- stamp duty if the purchase price is over £30,000
- deposit or rent in advance on a flat.

If you are selling your old home, splitting the proceeds and both buying new homes, you will probably have to pay

○ three sets of conveyancing fees: one sale and two purchases
○ two sets of surveyor's valuation fees (if you are both going to take out new mortgages) and structural survey fees
○ bridging finance on one or both properties
○ two items of stamp duty if houses each cost over £30,000
○ estate agent's commission on the sale of your old home
○ two sets of mortgagee's solicitors' fees
○ two sets of removal charges (even if one of you is moving into rented accommodation, there may be removal expenses)
○ for new carpets, curtains and general redecoration in one or both new homes.

If there is no suitable accommodation in the area (either because buying is too expensive or there is no rented accommodation available), this may involve increased travelling costs to work for whoever has moved out.

### changed costs of living

Unless you are a two-car family, one of you is going to lose the use of what was the family car. Not only may this involve additional expense in using a public transport, but it can also be considerably inconvenient – for example, if you used the car to run the children to school.

Food is not such a substantial item as accommodation, but it may nevertheless cause additional expense. A man now living on his own, for example, not used to cooking for himself, may feed himself uneconomically by eating out, or buying prepared convenience foods.

During the course of your marriage, both of you will have done many unpaid tasks around the house which you may not now have time or ability to do for yourself. For example, you may have to employ somebody to do the cleaning, washing and ironing, or pay someone to do various do-it-yourself jobs around the house.

For the parent who has moved out, seeing the children may involve substantial travelling costs (for them to visit you or you to go to them) and extra expense on outings, especially if it is not practical to have them to stay. The one who has moved out may also feel a need, especially in the early stages, to buy the children extra, compensatory, treats.

Generally speaking, in financial terms you may find that you have lost more than you have gained. But this may be more than made up for by release from a relationship that has become an intolerable burden to one or both of you.

# GETTING A DIVORCE

The sole ground for a divorce in England or Wales is the irretrievable breakdown of the marriage. A marriage cannot, however, be held to have broken down irretrievably unless the petitioner satisfies the divorce court of one or more of the following facts

1 that the respondent has committed adultery and the petitioner finds it intolerable to live with the respondent
2 that the respondent has behaved in such a way that the petitioner cannot reasonably be expected to live with the respondent
3 that the respondent has deserted the petitioner for a continuous period of at least two years immediately preceding the presentation of the petition
4 that the parties have lived apart for a continuous period of at least two years immediately preceding the presentation of the petition and that the respondent consents to a decree being granted
5 that the parties have lived apart for a continuous period of at least five years immediately preceding the presentation of the petition.

A petition for divorce cannot be presented until one year after the marriage took place, whatever exceptional circumstances there may be. Judicial separation proceedings may be commenced at any time after the marriage.

A decree of divorce cannot be made absolute or a decree of judicial separation will not be granted unless the arrangements for children of the family are declared by the court to be satisfactory or the best that can be devised in the circumstances.

Where you got married, whether in this country or abroad, is not relevant in determining whether an english court has 'jurisdiction' to hear your petition, but either you or your spouse must be domiciled in England or Wales or have been resident there for at least one year before the date of presenting the petition. Short absences (for example, for holidays) can be ignored.

It is advisable to consult a solicitor straightaway in connection with any proposed divorce where there is doubt about domicile or when neither of the couple lives in England or Wales.

Domicile or residence in Scotland, Northern Ireland, the Channel Islands, the Isle of Man is not sufficient to enable a petition for divorce to be made in an english court.

## judicial separation

A petition for a decree of judicial separation can be presented at any time after marriage and makes it possible for a spouse to get a court order for financial or property provision. The effect of a decree is that the petitioner is technically relieved of the obligation to reside with the respondent but, in law, the couple remain married, so neither can marry anyone else and on the death of one partner, the other would be his or her widow or widower. This can be particularly important in the case of an elderly couple when a wife would lose substantial widow's pension benefits on divorce. The decree does, however, affect inheritance rights if either spouse dies without having made a will.

A decree of judicial separation does not preclude a divorce later and the fact relied on to obtain the original decree may be relied on in the later divorce proceedings and does not have to be re-proved, but there is then the added ingredient of 'irretrievable breakdown'. The procedure for obtaining a decree of judicial separation is similar to divorce but there is only one decree, with no interim stage.

# the procedure

Whichever of a couple formally initiates the divorce is called the petitioner, the other is the respondent.

One of you has to be petitioner and the other respondent, and you should try to avoid coming to blows over who is going to file the petition. There is, however, a practical advantage in being the petitioner because it is the petitioner who is in the driving seat and who can to some extent control the pace of the divorce.

You can choose which of you is going to file the petition and on what grounds but it is not possible to file a petition jointly. The history of divorce law stems from the idea of a 'matrimonial offence' and this legacy still lingers in some of the 'facts' which have to be proved to secure a decree. Some people find offensive the idea of being the respondent and admitting adultery or unreasonable behaviour. It will not, however, affect how a court decides related issues to do with money or the children, unless the petitioner specifically alleges in those related proceedings that the other's conduct has been so bad that it should be taken into account.

In an undefended case, a solicitor is not needed for the actual procedure of getting divorced. However, you may want advice from a solicitor before embarking on divorce proceedings. You may want to check whether there are grounds for divorce in your case and that you unde. land what has to be done, by whom and when, and what the implications are of the questions you will be required to answer on the various forms that have to be completed and submitted to the court. It is useful also to get some advice on financial matters at an early stage.

Undefended divorce is dealt with by the 'special procedure' system with no hearing in open court in respect of the divorce petition itself, but there will be a short appointment before a judge to check that the arrangements for the children are satisfactory. The facts in the petition (and subsequent affidavit) are considered by the registrar of the divorce court without either spouse being present.

**documents needed**

To start divorce proceedings, the following will be needed

○ the completed form of petition for divorce, with a copy for the other spouse (the respondent) plus an extra copy in an adultery case where the co-respondent is named

○ the marriage certificate or a certified copy of it.

A photocopy of the marriage certificate is not acceptable. A certified copy can be obtained, for a fee, from the General Register Office, St Catherines House, 10 Kingsway, London WC2B 6JP, or from the superintendent registrar of births, deaths and marriages for the district or the incumbent of the church where the marriage took place. (The marriage certificate will not be returned to you after the divorce.) If your marriage certificate is in a foreign language, you will also need a formal translation of it.

○ a fee of £40 (or a completed fees-exemption form if you are exempted because you are receiving supplementary benefit or family income supplement, or legal advice under the green form scheme)

○ a statement of the proposed arrangements for any relevant children, with a copy for the other spouse.

Forms for the petition and for the statement of arrangements for children are available from divorce court offices and the Divorce Registry, without charge, and also a free booklet *Undefended divorce – a guide for the petitioner acting without a solicitor*. In some courts, the staff will help you complete the forms but they are not allowed to give you legal advice.

Whichever spouse is the petitioner sends or takes the papers to any divorce county court or to the Divorce Registry in London (Somerset House, Strand, London WC2R 1LP). Not all county courts deal with divorces; check with your local one (listed under 'courts' in the telephone directory).

You should keep a copy for yourself of any document that you supply to the court or to the other spouse.

A reference number will be allocated to your petition by the court and must be quoted on all communications to the court throughout the case.

## the petition

There is a standard printed form of petition for each of the five facts, obtainable from the divorce court office or the Divorce Registry. With the form of petition, the court supplies notes for guidance which you should read carefully before completing your petition.

In the petition, you must give the date and place of the marriage (which must be copied exactly from the certificate); the address at which you and your spouse last lived together and your present address(es); the occupations of yourself and spouse; the names and dates of birth of children; details of any previous court proceedings relating to the marriage or property.

The form assumes that the petitioner is domiciled in England or Wales; if you are not, you must make clear that you are relying on your spouse's domicile or the 'habitual residence' provisions (at least one year in England or Wales).

You must set out one or more of the five facts on which you rely to show that the marriage has irretrievably broken down. Eventually you will have to give evidence of the facts, normally by affidavit (a sworn statement).

It is important to complete the form of petition accurately. If you are unsure, and the court office is unable to assist, you should consult a solicitor.

### fact 1 *adultery and intolerability*

In the petition, no more need be said than that the respondent has committed adultery with the co-respondent (whose identity or name and address must be given, if known).

You are asked to say when and where adultery has taken place so far as you know. If your spouse provides a confession statement admitting adultery at a specific time and place with a person whose name, address and identity he or she refuses to disclose, such a statement will be accepted and you can copy the details given on to the petition. No third party will then be involved in the proceedings. If, however, you do in fact know who the person is, you have a duty to name him or her as the co-respondent. Mere suspicion is not knowledge but an incorrect assertion that you do not know could lead to the decree being rescinded.

The petitioner must, in addition, state that he or she finds it intolerable to live with the other spouse. (A petitioner in Scotland or Northern Ireland has to prove the respondent's adultery only and not that he or she also finds it intolerable to live with the respondent.)

### fact 2 *unreasonable behaviour*
There is no simple definition of unreasonable behaviour. The law says 'that the respondent has behaved in such a way that the petitioner cannot reasonably be expected to live with the respondent'. Violence or serious threats of violence to the petitioner or to the children, homosexual conduct, persistent nagging, refusal to have sexual intercourse or to have children knowing that the other spouse wished to have them, financial irresponsibility such as gambling to excess, other persistent extravagance to the detriment of the family's welfare – are some examples of what can amount to unreasonable behaviour. Even behaviour caused by insanity is taken into account, but many less grave matters are sufficient.

The test is whether the court feels that between the particular husband and wife the behaviour complained of is sufficiently serious to make it unreasonable to expect the petitioner to go on living with the respondent. Usually there will have to have been a number of incidents evidencing the breakdown of the marriage. Mere incompatibility is not enough, unless it has driven one or both partners to behave unreasonably – for example, by showing no sexual interest or affection, being abusive and derogatory, and so on.

If the behaviour of one of the spouses has forced the other to leave home, this would be evidence of the unreasonableness of the behaviour.

In the petition, you should set out a fairly precise account of the alleged behaviour, giving details, with the approximate dates and places preferably in date order, of incidents of importance that led to the breakdown of the marriage, so that the respondent can know what is alleged and the court can decide whether the behaviour was unreasonable. Try to be concise – several short paragraphs giving the bare bones of the allegations will usually be sufficient.

If you have continued to live together, it is particularly important that details of incidents of unreasonable behaviour within the last six months are included in the petition. Further evidence can, if necessary, be given in the affidavit that follows the petition.

*fact 3 desertion*
Desertion as the basis for divorce means a period of separation of at least two years brought about by husband or wife leaving the other against the other one's wishes. You have to state the circumstances, the date when he or she left, and that it was without your consent.

*facts 4 and 5 separation*
In order to establish separation as proof of the breakdown of a marriage, a couple must have lived apart for at least two years if the respondent consents to the divorce, or for more than five years if there is no consent. The date of separation should be stated in the petition as accurately as possible.

If the separation has been for more than two but less than five years, the respondent's positive consent to being divorced is necessary – not just lack of objection. After five or more years' separation, the respondent's consent is not required (but there is provision for opposing on the grounds that the divorce would cause grave financial or other hardship).

In all separation cases, the respondent may request that his or her future financial position be considered by the court before the decree is made final. The respondent's financial position as a result of being divorced will then be closely scrutinised and the petitioner will have to safeguard the respondent's position in order to obtain a decree.

## six months for attempted reconciliation
On the affidavit that has to follow the petition, there are questions about times when the couple have lived in the same household. To allow for attempts at reconciliation, you can have gone on living together for a period of up to six months, or several shorter periods which together add up to not more than six months, without affecting the facts on which the petition is based.

### *after adultery*
After a petitioner became aware of the other's adultery, a period of living together which has exceeded six months by the time the decree nisi stage has been reached (or even the stage of applying for the decree to be made absolute) would prevent a decree, even though the period may have been less than six months at the date of the petition.

Time begins to run only from the date that you knew of the actual adultery referred to in the petition. Thus, for example, if you had suspected that your spouse had been having an affair, approached him or her and, as a result, a confession was then made (in the form, perhaps, of a written confession statement), you can state that you 'knew' only from the date of the confession, even if adultery had taken place some while ago.

### *after unreasonable behaviour*
Where unreasonable behaviour is alleged in the petition, the period of living together is counted from the last act of unreasonable behaviour and will be taken into account in deciding whether the petitioner can reasonably be expected to live with the respondent.

Living together for more than six months would not necessarily prevent a decree being granted, but the court would require a detailed explanation and may well conclude that the respondent's behaviour was not unreasonable.

*after separation*

Although periods of living together totalling not more than six months since separation or desertion will not invalidate the divorce petition, any such period will not count as part of the two-year or five-year threshold. For instance, if you have lived together for three months in an attempt at reconciliation (which has failed) and then parted again, the petition cannot be filed until two years and three months and one day have elapsed since the original separation.

## the 'prayer'

The last page of the petition contains the petitioner's formal request (prayer) that the marriage be dissolved.

This is the place for the petitioner also to ask for custody of children; for the costs of the case to be paid by the respondent and/or co-respondent; and, under the heading of 'ancillary relief', for orders for maintenance (called periodical payments), lump sum payments and property adjustment.

It is better not to cross anything off the list of requests, because it may be complicated or even impossible to apply later, but do not specify any actual amounts at this stage.

If the requests are not left standing in the prayer, the petitioner would have to make a special application to the court for leave to apply later for any required order. Such an application is not certain to be granted if it is made after a long time lag or if, for example, the respondent said that he or she decided not to defend the petition only because of the absence of any request for ancillary relief.

If you have agreed with your spouse that no financial claims will be made, you should include them in the petition nevertheless so that they can be formally dismissed (only if claims have been made can they be dismissed). But to avoid misunderstanding and distress when your spouse receives the petition, explain that the claims are being included only to be dismissed. Similarly, you can include a prayer for costs even though you may agree (or decide) not to follow this request through.

What you are claiming is costs only in respect of the divorce itself (not ancillary issues such as finance or custody) and these costs will be comparatively low. It is also possible to seek costs against a co-respondent, but it would be wise to discuss this with a solicitor.

If you have agreed with your spouse that you will have joint custody of the children, or if you want to share custody with your spouse even if not suggesting that the children should live with you, add in the prayer that you are seeking custody 'jointly with the respondent'.

---

<u>PRAYER</u>

The petitioner therefore prays:—

(1) That the said marriage be dissolved.

(2) That the petitioner may be granted the custody of

(3) That the           may be ordered to pay the costs of this suit.

(4) That the petitioner may be granted the following ancillary relief:
  (a) an order for maintenance pending suit
     a periodical payments order
     a secured provision order
     a lump sum order

  (b) a periodical payments order
     a secured provision order   } for the children of the family
     a lump sum order

  (c) a property adjustment order

Signed

The names and addressed of the persons to be served with this petition are:—

Respondent:—

Co-Respondent (adultery case only):—

The Petitioner's address for service is:—

Dated this      day of      19

Address all communications for the court to: The Chief Clerk, County Court,

The Court }
office at   }

is open from 10 a.m. to 4 p.m. (4.30 p.m. at the Divorce Registry) on Mondays to Fridays.

**statement as to arrangements for children**

All children of the family, whatever their age, have to be named in the petition. 'Children of the family' are, in broad terms, children who are children of both husband and wife, children adopted by them both, step-children, and other children who have been treated at any time during the marriage by both as part of the family – but not foster-children.

A statement about the proposed arrangements for relevant children must be signed by the petitioner and sent (plus a copy for the other spouse) with the petition. (A printed form of statement is available from the court office.)

Relevant children are those under the age of 16, or under the age of 18 and receiving instruction at an educational establishment or undergoing training for a trade, profession or vocation (even if the child is also earning). If a child over 16 and under 18 is not still being educated or trained, it is important to say so in the petition.

Among the particulars to be given in the statement is information about where each child is to live, including details of the accommodation, names of other persons living there and who will look after the children. Details of financial provision have to be given, stating who is at present supporting the children, and whether an application will be made to the court for an order for their financial support.

The name of the school or other educational establishment which each child does or will attend has to be given or, if he is working, his place of employment, the nature of his work and of any training he will receive.

You are also asked to state any agreed access arrangements or the extent to which access will be given. Often all that is stated is 'reasonable access is sought/will be given'.

Although courts like these statements to be as comprehensive as possible, it may be difficult to give detailed information about proposed arrangements which are likely not to be known at this stage, and simply setting out your wishes could be contentious. It may be better, therefore, just to give details of present arrangements and any specific plans for the future, and explain that, for example, the children's future accommodation has yet to be decided.

## service of the petition

The court sends to the respondent, at the address given in the petition, one copy of the petition and of the statement of the arrangements for any children.

The court also sends an 'acknowledgment of service' form, which the respondent must complete and return to the court within 8 days. (If adultery is alleged and a co-respondent is named, a copy of the petition is sent to him or her, also with an acknowledgment of service form to be returned to the court.)

The petition is normally posted by the court to the respondent. Service is proved by the return of the acknowledgment of service form to the court. If the acknowledgment of service is not returned, the petitioner can apply to the court for a fresh set of documents and arrange for personal service.

Personal service by the petitioner is not permitted. The petitioner can apply to the registrar for an order that the petition be served by the bailiff of the county court for the area in which the respondent lives, or can employ an enquiry agent to act as process server.

When the respondent fails to return the acknowledgment of service but has acted in a way which makes it clear that he or she has received the petition, an application can be made by the petitioner for service of the petition to be deemed to have been effected.

If service is, in practice, not possible, the petitioner may be able to get a court order dispensing with service.

### the respondent responding

With the documents sent to the respondent is an explanatory leaflet called 'Notice of proceedings' telling the respondent some of the implications of the answers he or she may give on the acknowledgment of service.

The acknowledgment of service is not only an acknowledgment that the petition has been received: it includes questions
about the respondent's intentions, such as whether he or she
wishes to defend, wishes to be heard on the matter of costs or
custody, or wishes to make an application for custody or access
on his or her own behalf.

If you do not dispute that the children should live with the
petitioner but you want to apply for joint custody, you should
specify this rather than just asking for 'custody', in order to
prevent any misunderstandings.

If you do not agree with the proposed arrangements, first
make sure that what you are objecting to are actual proposals
and not mere 'wishes'. Try to discuss them with your spouse.
If there is underlying disagreement, send to the court your
counter proposals, preferably setting them out in a similar
format.

If a prayer for costs has been made in the petition, you are
asked whether you object to paying the petitioner's costs. If
you do object, you are asked to explain why. You may, for
example, have agreed with the petitioner not to pursue costs
against you, and your comment to this effect should remind
him or her to delete that request from the affidavit following
the petition.

In an adultery case, the respondent is asked to indicate if he
or she admits adultery and to sign the acknowledgment of
service even if a solicitor is also signing.

In a separation case, the respondent has to reply to the
question on the acknowledgment of service form whether he
or she intends to apply for the court to consider the financial
position as it will be after the divorce.

Where it is a separation with consent, the respondent has to
confirm consent by saying 'yes' and also putting his or her
signature on the form.

All financial matters and arrangements for children are dealt
with as separate issues, irrespective of whether the divorce
itself is defended or undefended.

*defending*

If the respondent does not agree that a divorce should be
obtained on the basis of the petition and wishes to defend, he
or she must file an 'answer' at the court. (Preparing an answer
should be done with the help of a solicitor.) It is important that
the respondent acts promptly. There are strict time limits: 8
days for filing an acknowledgment of service, 29 days (from
receipt of the petition) for filing an answer. It is possible to file
an answer without having given 'notice of intention to defend'
on the acknowledgment of service but in order to ensure that
he or she gets the full 29 days in which to prepare an answer,
the respondent should give 'notice of intention' in the acknowledgment. It may be possible to obtain special leave from the
court to file an answer out of time, but only if there was a very
good reason. If you are in any doubt, you should consult a
solicitor at once. (In Scotland, different time limits apply.)

Although many respondents feel hurt and angry when the
petition arrives and in no mood to concede, very few divorce
petitions are actually defended. The cost of fighting over the
decree is prodigious.

If you accept that the marriage is over but object to some or
all of the allegations made, try to discuss these together as
calmly as possible. Once your spouse knows that you will not
object to the divorce itself, he or she might be willing to amend
the petition so that it is less offensive, and so that there is
minimal risk of the allegations being treated as relevant conduct in financial proceedings.

Allegations made in a 'behaviour' petition, designed to be
just sufficient to secure a decree, could be bolstered up later if
the petitioner wished to argue that conduct should be taken
into account in the financial proceedings. With the prospect of
conduct being raised in financial applications (albeit probably
not successfully), the effect of not challenging a behaviour
petition should not be treated too cavalierly. But if conduct is
not to be relied on in the financial proceedings, not defending
should not prejudice you.

If a behaviour petition is undefended, the respondent cannot subsequently – for example, in the financial proceedings – deny the allegations, but he or she can deny (a) that they represent the full story and (b) that of themselves they justify greater or lesser financial provision than would otherwise have been the case.

After an answer and any reply to the answer have been filed, the registrar usually fixes an appointment in his chambers when both parties (with their solicitors if they are represented) will be required to attend. Courts go out of their way to discourage defended petitions and the registrar will see if there is any way of avoiding a defended divorce. Only if these efforts fail will the registrar allow the case to go forward to a hearing.

The hearing will be in open court before a judge. A defended divorce would need a solicitor for each spouse and may also need the services of barristers when it gets to court.

If, however, the respondent files an answer not denying the allegations but seeking a divorce on other facts, and the petitioner does not dispute the cross-petition, the divorce is not treated as defended and the special procedure can be adopted.

It is also possible to obtain cross-decrees. Sometimes initially defended proceedings can be 'compromised' by the petitioner obtaining a decree on the basis of the petition and the respondent on the basis of the answer.

## getting back together

Some couples, once the divorce procedure is well under way find that there is a chance of saving the marriage but feel they are bound to continue with the court action to the end. This is not necessary. If you think at any stage that you and your husband/wife might like to give the marriage another try, you are quite free to do so; it is best to tell your solicitor and the court what is happening. You can apply to the court to dismiss the petition when you feel the reconciliation is working. Where there has been an injunction 'ousting' your spouse from the home, however, allowing him or her to return without asking the court to discharge the injunction could amount to contempt of court even if both of you agree that the move back should be made.

You may want to consider whether some or all of the differences with your spouse can be resolved with outside, non-legal, help. A fresh viewpoint can often be useful. Such help can be obtained from a marriage guidance council or a conciliation service (your citizens advice bureau will know where such agencies are). More and more emphasis nowadays is placed on conciliation – trying to help the couple to resolve as many problems as possible by mutual agreement or mediation.

## applying for 'directions for trial'

The court sends a copy of the respondent's acknowledgment of service to the petitioner, who can then apply for 'directions for trial' – that is, make a written request that the case be given a date for the decree nisi to be pronounced.

You can only apply for directions for trial if you can prove that the respondent, and any co-respondent, have been served with the petition, and have had the opportunity to defend it.

The appropriate documents are normally sent to the petitioner by the court office when it has received the acknowledgment of service from the respondent.

The petitioner must complete and lodge with the court one copy of a form 'Request for directions for trial (special procedure)' and an affidavit in support, with the copy of the acknowledgment of service attached. You should fill in only the top part of the request form: the name of the court, the number assigned to the petition, the names of the petitioner and respondent; then date and sign it. The rest of the form is completed by the registrar and court staff.

### affidavits

The 'special procedure' affidavit is a fairly straightforward document, mostly in the form of a questionnaire. The questions refer to the petition, asking for confirmation that its contents are true, and for any alterations or additions. (Do not forget that giving false information is perjury.) You also have to state whether you are going to pursue any requests for costs made in the prayer of the petition.

There is a different affidavit of evidence for each of the five facts on which a divorce can be based. If you want to rely on two facts – for example, unreasonable behaviour and adultery – two affidavits would have to be completed.

### *affidavit on adultery*

You are asked to state the facts on which you base the allegation of adultery. You should refer to the relevant numbered paragraphs in the petition and state that the allegations are true to the best of your knowledge and belief.

If the respondent has admitted the adultery on the acknowledgment of service or by making a written confession statement, you should identify the respondent's signature on the document, which should be sent with (exhibited to) the affidavit; similarly, if the co-respondent has supplied a confession statement. The co-respondent does not need to have admitted the adultery for the divorce to go through, provided that the respondent has made the admission or the petitioner can prove the adultery.

If the adultery has not been admitted by the respondent (and provided that you can prove service of the petition on the respondent and co-respondent), you should give all the firsthand information available, such as the date of confession of adultery or details of circumstances that tend to show that the respondent has committed adultery. 'Hearsay' evidence that you have been told by other people that your husband/wife has been committing adultery is not acceptable, and you may need to supply further affidavits by other people who can give corroborative information.

You also have to confirm that you find it intolerable to live with the respondent.

*affidavit on unreasonable behaviour*
Further evidence to substantiate any allegations made in the petition may be given. But there is no need for a blow-by-blow account of every incident, provided that the respondent's conduct has been adequately set out in the petition. If the registrar is not satisfied with the information given, he will call for further evidence to be supplied, such as a medical report or a witness's affidavit.

In order to clarify whether, and for how long, you have gone on living with the respondent, you are specifically asked whether the behaviour described in the petition is continuing and, if not, when the last incident relied on took place. You then have to say whether you have lived at the same address for more than six months since then and, if so, you have to describe what arrangements you had for sharing the accommodation. This involves giving details of sleeping, cooking and cleaning arrangements.

### affidavit on desertion

The date on which desertion began has to be given, and you must state that you did not agree to the separation and that he or she did not offer to return.

### affidavit on separation

Where you and your spouse have been living in separate households for the whole of the period apart, the relevant dates and separate addresses should be given, and when and why you decided that the marriage was at an end. Merely living apart is not necessarily sufficient; the separation starts from the time you considered the marriage had broken down.

You are asked to say when you came to the conclusion that the marriage was at an end – not when you decided to get divorced, which could well have been at a much later date.

You may have had to continue living at the same address because it was impossible or impracticable to live completely apart, although the marriage was at an end. You may not consider that you have been 'living together' if you have merely been under the same roof and, for example, sleeping separately, not having sexual intercourse, and barely communicating but a court could hold that you have in fact been living together in one, unhappy, household. The court needs to be convinced that there were, to all intents and purposes, two households, if you are not to be treated as having been living together. In such a case, you must give the fullest possible information about the separateness of the households. If the space provided in the standard affidavit form is inadequate, attach an extra sheet dealing with this point.

If the registrar is still in doubt about the circumstances, he may remove the case from the special procedure list, to be heard in open court, so that fuller evidence can be given. If this happens, you may need to consult a solicitor; you can apply for legal aid to be represented at the hearing if your financial position makes you eligible.

*completing the affidavit*

You must return with the affidavit the copy of the respondent's acknowledgment of service form sent by the court, and identify the signature on it as being that of the respondent. The statement in the affidavit should be completed by inserting the respondent's name exactly as he or she has signed the acknowledgment of service i.e. *L. F. Smith* not Lawrence Frederick Smith. In a divorce with consent, this signature proves the respondent's consent to the divorce.

An affidavit is sworn by taking it to a commissioner for oaths or a solicitor (but not the one acting for the person swearing the affidavit) or the court office. There is no fee for swearing an affidavit before a court official; a solicitor or commissioner for oaths makes a small charge (at present, £3 plus 75p per exhibit – any document attached).

When the completed affidavit has been signed and sworn, it has to be sent or taken to the court with the application form requesting directions for trial.

**registrar giving directions**

Provided that the registrar is satisfied as to service of the petition on everybody concerned and that they have had the opportunity of defending, and in a 'consent' case that the respondent's consent has been filed, he gives directions for the case to be entered in the special procedure list.

If the registrar is not satisfied with the information in the affidavit, he may invite the petitioner (or a witness) to file a further affidavit or to give additional information on the points the registrar is concerned about.

If the registrar still does not accept that there is sufficient evidence for a divorce, he may direct that the petition be removed from the special procedure list. A fresh application then has to be made for directions and for a date to be fixed for a hearing in open court before a judge.

When the registrar is satisfied that there is sufficient evidence to support the petition, he certifies that the petitioner is entitled to a decree nisi of divorce (or the decree of judicial separation). The court then fixes a date for the judge to pronounce the decree nisi.

## decree nisi and decree absolute

The decree nisi is a provisional decree and does not dissolve the marriage. It entitles the one who was the petitioner to apply to the court for the decree to be made absolute after six weeks have elapsed. Until this is done, you are still married.

The form of application for the decree nisi to be made absolute has to be obtained from the court office; it should be completed and returned to the court six weeks after decree nisi. There is a fee of £10.

A decree can be made absolute earlier than the six weeks if the petitioner applies for this when the decree nisi is pronounced and attends to explain to the judge in person the reason for the application. The respondent must be given notice of this application by the petitioner. Such an application might be granted, for example, to enable one of the couple to marry again before a child is born.

If the petitioner does not apply for the decree nisi to be made absolute when the time comes, after a further three months have elapsed (that is, three calendar months and six weeks after the decree nisi), the person who was the respondent may apply to the registrar for the decree to be made absolute, with an affidavit setting out the reasons why it is he or she who is applying rather than the petitioner.

If decree absolute has not been applied for within 12 months of decree nisi, an explanation must be lodged with the application for decree absolute, giving the reason for the delay, and stating whether the couple have cohabited since decree nisi and whether any further children have been born to the wife (and if so, whether it is alleged that it is a child of the family, in which case the registrar must refer the matter to the judge, to consider the arrangements for the child). A registrar may require further explanation or even affidavit evidence before the decree is made absolute.

The certificate making the decree absolute is sent by the court office to both parties. The certificate may be ready as quickly as the next day. From the date on it, the marriage is at an end in law. Keep this certificate carefully; it will have to be produced if you want to marry again. Make a note of the name of the court, the reference number of the case and the date of the decree.

Some overseas countries do not like the relative informality of our decrees absolute, so if you are planning to live outside the UK, you may need a certified copy of the decree absolute, signed by the registrar and stamped by the court, which may be more easily accepted. It is wise also to check whether the certificate should be notarised by the embassy in the UK of the country in which you plan to remarry.

If a divorced Jew wishes to marry again in an Orthodox synagogue, a religious bill of divorcement, known as a Get, must be obtained from the jewish religious authorities (the Beth Din) in addition to a civil decree from a court of law. Under circumstances in which it is impossible for the husband to deliver the Get personally to his wife, he may designate a messenger to act as proxy for him. (Special rules for preparing and delivering a Get by messenger must be followed.) The divorced woman is free to contract marriage then. She cannot, however, marry the man suspected of having committed adultery with her and she cannot marry within three months after divorce. The Liberal synagogue will accept, instead of a Get, a written declaration from the divorced other partner that an application for a Get would not be opposed.

# ARRANGEMENTS FOR THE CHILDREN

Divorce is a decision reached by adults and often comes as a great shock to children, even when to their parents the strains in the marriage have become only too clear. The instinctive reaction of a child may be similar to your own or your spouse's immediate reaction – disbelief, denial and a frantic attempt to make it not happen. It is important that you find time to allay fears by explaining what is happening and by providing reassurance. This can be far from easy when you yourself are in a state of emotional turmoil and stress.

When you are trying to put the past behind you and start a new life, it may be difficult to accept that your children's needs are different from yours and may even conflict with yours to some extent. For example, children often say very little about wanting to see the parent who has left home because they are aware that this may upset the parent they are living with. Their silence does not mean that they are not missing the other parent. Both parents need to reassure the children that they do not have to choose one and reject the other, and that their separation is in no way the children's fault.

Your status as a husband or wife will come to an abrupt end on pronouncement of decree absolute. The same is not true of your status as a parent. Moreover, your relationship with your former spouse should continue in some shape or form so long as you have children.

A fundamental issue is how the children are going to keep in touch with the parent with whom they are not living. Working out access arrangements that both parents can cope with takes a lot of effort and the potential for disagreement is obvious. Be careful, however, to avoid playing out in the guise of disputes over access what are really matrimonial disputes. Also, be aware of the fact that your former spouse is likely to behave in the same kinds of irritating ways that he or she did while you were married – and the same will probably be true of you. So, you will both need to behave with greater consideration than before.

Sorting out arrangements concerning the children will be a continuing process but it is one that gets increasingly easier – as emotions die down, as the children get older and as a routine becomes established. Initially, you may find great difficulty even in discussing proposed arrangements with your former spouse. At this stage, bear in mind the possibility of conciliation. This is a word easily confused with reconciliation, but they are two quite different concepts. Reconciliation means that a couple have got back together as husband and wife, conciliation is a process designed to help them settle their differences amicably, but in the context of their separation.

## conciliation

The function of conciliation is to assist separating spouses to work out for themselves a solution of their difficulties which will be mutually acceptable. In other words, the activity is one of mediation with no pressure exercised to agree to any particular solution.

By meeting in a neutral environment in the presence of a non-partisan, experienced professional who is specially trained in assisting couples to come to realistic agreements, you may find that you and your spouse can at least (and perhaps at last) communicate directly rather than talking at or over each other or entirely missing each other's points. Parents are encouraged to find solutions in respect of arrangements for their children which are mutually acceptable and which enable them to remain parents in as full a sense as possible. In doing this, the conciliator will not try to impose any outcome of his or her own choice but will try to help you and your partner find common ground. He or she does, however, exercise control over how you try to reach an agreement and, for example, will try to ensure that each of you is allowed by the other to make your views clear. Discussions are confidential and are not to be referred to if there is subsequent litigation. Also, if you do not wish to disclose your address to your spouse, this wish will be respected.

There is an increasing number of family conciliation services of which many are affiliated to the National Family Conciliation Council. The local citizens advice bureau will be able to give you the address of your nearest service, or write to the NFCC (enclosing a stamped addressed envelope) at 34 Milton Road, Swindon, Wiltshire SN1 5JA. The NFCC code of practice says

". . . Conciliation is a process which requires the co-operation of both parties, and which respects their autonomy and legal rights. The conciliator helps the parties to explore possibilities of reaching agreement, without coercion. Where children are involved, the conciliator helps the parties to work out arrangements which balance their individual interests with those of their children. . . . Conciliation may include preliminary discussions about issues of finance and property where these cannot be separated from the primary issues about the divorce and/or children. . . ."

Divorce proceedings need not have been started for conciliation to be a possibility and conciliation remains a possibility even if the divorce itself was some time ago. It is not a cure-all but an additional resource open to you. If you do not achieve a settlement, you can invoke the aid of the court to seek a formal decision on the issue in question.

### appointment with judge about children

A date will be fixed for the judge to decide whether the arrangements proposed are satisfactory. This is usually, but not necessarily, on the same day as the decree nisi is to be pronounced.

The notice giving you the date of decree nisi also gives the time and place of the 'children's appointment' or tells you that you should apply separately for this. In a case of judicial separation, the children's hearing must precede the pronouncement of the decree, even if only by minutes.

Both parents are notified by the court of the date. The petitioner normally has to attend and the respondent must do so if the children will be living with him or her, or may have to if there is an application for joint custody. Some courts require both parents to attend in any event to see if there are any problems that require sorting out. Although it is referred to as the 'children's appointment', the children do not attend.

Take to the appointment at the court a copy of the petition and of the statement of the proposed arrangements, and also any relevant documents, such as a copy of any previous court order for custody.

The hearing is in chambers – that is, in a court room in private – and is relatively informal, with the judge and clerk, the parents and their legal advisers (if any) and perhaps the court welfare officer present. The judge may ask questions about any points – for instance, he will want to know that there are proper arrangements for the children to see the parent with whom they are not based; that adequate financial provision is being made for the children; that the children get on reasonably well with any cohabitant of the parent with whom they will live.

If the judge is not satisfied, he adjourns the hearing and may ask for further information or for a report from the court welfare officer.

If there is no agreement between the parents about where the children are to live or access arrangements, the judge will not deal with the question at the children's appointment but may give directions – for example, about the filing of affidavits by each parent – or may refer them to an in-court conciliation service. Or the judge may order a court welfare officer to prepare a report if he thinks this would be helpful. The welfare officer's report would set out the facts and circumstances and his or her impressions, and generally includes a recommendation to which the court would pay great attention (although not necessarily follow).

(In Scotland, there is no children's appointment with a judge and no certificate of satisfaction is required.)

**certificate of satisfaction about children**

No decree of judicial separation or decree absolute of divorce can be made where there are relevant children unless the judge has certified his satisfaction declaring

o that the arrangements that have been made for every relevant child are satisfactory or are the best that can be devised under the circumstances

> *or*

o that it is impracticable for the parents to make such arrangements (for instance, if the children are living abroad)

> *or*

o that there are circumstances making it desirable that the decree should be granted or made absolute without delay, even though the judge is unable to make the required declaration about the children. One parent (or both) must give the court a satisfactory undertaking to bring the question of the arrangements for the children before the court within a time specified by the judge.

The judge may in some circumstances feel able to give a 'certificate of satisfaction' even though there are outstanding issues of custody, care and control or access, but this would depend on the particular case.

Where there are difficulties about the arrangements for the children, these must be sorted out before a decree nisi can be made absolute.

When the judge is satisfied, he records his 'certificate of satisfaction' and issues the necessary orders.

Generally, parents seek orders about custody, about care and control and about access. If these are agreed, orders will usually be made as requested. It is rare for a judge to refuse to make an order which both parents want unless the proposed arrangements seem entirely unsatisfactory – in which case, a certificate of satisfaction will not have been given.

# court orders about children

In the petition, the petitioner can request custody of any children of the family, and the respondent is asked in the acknowledgment of service whether he or she objects and wishes to make an application for custody on his or her own account.

The orders made by the court on divorce are generally three-fold: an order for custody, an order for care and control, an order for access.

**Custody** is a term indicating the right to make major, long term decisions for a child, primarily in respect of education, medical care, moral and religious up-bringing, marriage and suchlike. The parent having **care and control** of a child is the parent with whom the child lives and it is he or she who has the right to make the practical everyday decisions about the child. The parent with care and control will almost invariably also have an order for custody in his or her favour. That custody order may be either an order for sole custody or an order for joint custody with the other parent. An **access** order confers the right of the parent with whom the child is not living to go on seeing the child.

## custody, care and control

Divorcing parents are increasingly encouraged to ask for a joint custody order where there is a prospect of the couple being able to co-operate as parents over their children in the future. For the parent with whom the children are not permanently based, a joint custody order gives legal recognition of his or her continuing parental role and parental obligations. It can accordingly have great symbolic value for both children and parents and can reduce the risk of one parent feeling that he or she has been 'judged' to be less caring or competent than the other. It does not, however, give him or her the right to interfere in day-to-day decision making and if there is a dispute between the parents over a major decision, such as a choice of school, the ultimate arbiter remains the court (as it also is when a parent without custody objects). The basis on which the court resolves any issue is what is in the child's best interests, not according to who has custody.

The key factor guiding the court in making all decisions in respect of children is this notion of the child's welfare. Every case is looked at individually in the light of all relevant circumstances. This 'welfare principle' takes precedence over every other factor so that the court will not be interested in who was to blame for breaking up a marriage, for example, unless that person's conduct seriously reflects on his or her abilities as a parent.

### resolving disputes

There is an increasing number of conciliation services organised by the courts themselves to which couples may be referred when there is a dispute about children. These 'in-court' services are run along broadly similar lines to the 'out-of-court' conciliation services, with the aim of helping two parents reach a solution in a supportive private setting acceptable to them both. The court welfare officer or other appointed conciliator talks with both parents and will be concerned to try to defuse the parents' competition to 'win' the children.

### *care and control*

There are certain common themes in resolving disputes about where the children should be based. For example, courts generally try to avoid splitting up brothers and sisters. If a child has become well-established with one parent, there would need to be very good reason for up-rooting him or her to go and live with the other parent. The ages and sex of the children are relevant – the older a child, particularly if a boy, the less the mother's initial advantage – and also such practical matters as who will look after the children when they get home from school and during the holidays. Depending on their ages, the children's wishes will be taken into account, but judges try to avoid putting children in the invidious position of having to choose between their parents.

## access

The parent who does not have care and control has the right (and, it is increasingly emphasised, the responsibility) to see the child. Very exceptional circumstances would be required to justify a court refusing to allow access.

If parents think that they will probably be able to sort out access arrangements themselves, the court usually makes an order for 'reasonable access', without specifying what this involves. What it does involve depends upon what you and your spouse agree, and this will depend upon your circumstances – how far apart you live, what your hours of work are, how old the children are and so on.

'Staying access' refers to access when the child stays with the parent overnight or for weekends, or for longer periods perhaps during school holidays. 'Visiting access' refers to visits by the parent when the child is generally collected and returned the same day; it does not mean that the access has to take place at the other parent's home.

A court can, however, be asked to specify what access a parent should have. Courts can make very specific orders stating dates, times, places and even when telephone calls may be made, but it is difficult for a court to ensure that access works well in practice.

Circumstances inevitably change and arrangements have to be reviewed from time to time in the light of such changes. What you are aiming at is the combination of flexibility and stability which best suits you, your spouse and, above all, your children. It is better to revise access arrangements by agreement rather than keep returning to court – and to get into the habit of reaching agreement as soon as possible.

## change of name

An order giving a parent custody or care and control specifically prohibits any step being taken which would result in the child being known by a new surname except with the leave of the court or the written consent of the other parent. In considering whether or not to give leave, the court would be guided by what is thought to be in the child's own best interests. (In Scotland, registering a change of name requires the consent of both parents.)

**undertaking to return children to England or Wales**
The order will also state that a parent may only arrange for the child to leave the court's jurisdiction within the UK if he or she has filed a written undertaking promising to return the child whenever called upon to do so by the court and has obtained the written consent of the other parent to the proposed trip. If you and your spouse are quite content to allow each other to take the children away for holidays in this way, you should each file an appropriate undertaking as soon as possible – it is easy to forget, if left. Clearly, any plans to emigrate would be quite a different matter.

If you have real fears that your spouse might not return the children, you should get a solicitor's advice without delay.

**emergencies**
Where there are grave difficulties which need urgent resolution, it may be essential to seek the assistance of the court. An interim hearing for a provisional order to be made can be obtained at short notice if necessary.

Wardship proceedings, which take effect instantly, are a further alternative if there is a threat, for example, that the child might be kidnapped. Taking or keeping your own child away from home without the explicit consent of the parent who has care and control, or 'disappearing' with the child if you have care and control, would lead to grave repercussions. Kidnapping is a criminal offence and is treated very seriously by the courts.

The Consumer Publication *Children, parents and the law* deals in more detail with wardship proceedings and abduction, as well as with orders for custody, care and control, access.

D.—3

# USING A SOLICITOR

'Do-it-yourself' divorce is relatively easy if you agree that there is to be a divorce and on what basis, but where financial arrangements and division of property and assets are in issue or where there is uncertainty about custody or access for children, a solicitor's help will almost certainly be needed. Some advice on the financial aspects from a solicitor specialising in divorce problems is worthwhile, if only to avoid giving up rights in ignorance.

If you can sort out your financial affairs as equal partners, so much the better although even then it is wise for you each to ask a solicitor whether the arrangements seem fair and to ensure that they are framed in as water-tight and tax-efficient a way as possible.

If it is not possible for the two of you to achieve a fair agreement on your own, one or both of you may need to use a solicitor to negotiate on your behalf. When faced with the breakdown of your marriage, you are likely to be at your most emotional, at the very time when you need to be as dispassionate and rational as possible.

Before you go to obtain legal advice, you should ask yourself what you are fighting for and why. Wanting a lawyer to act for you in a contentious way will involve you in expense, which may be out of proportion to anything gained. A solicitor can be of great help, but try to use his or her services efficiently and economically. The higher the costs the less there is left for you and your spouse and your children to share.

## why are you going to a solicitor?

Many people are not quite sure what they want from a solicitor. On the one hand, they want a fair and detached legal adviser, and on the other hand they want a knight in shining armour, a champion to wage war against their husband or wife.

Before you go to a solicitor, ask yourself 'what do I expect?'. Do not go for the following reasons:

*not in search of miracles*
There is no such thing as a magic answer. In many cases, there is not much room to manoeuvre: it is usually just a question of trying to make the best of what money and property there is.

*not just for emotional support*
Solicitors are often used as a shoulder to cry on. The one-to-one relationship, and client confidentiality, make them uniquely available for unburdening the soul. Many solicitors are very understanding and can be of great help at this time. But beware of reaching the stage where your solicitor becomes an emotional prop and you are not really telephoning to discuss the case but for personal reassurance. Apart from anything else, solicitors' time costs money: their job is to deal primarily with the legal aspects of your case.

*not for revenge*
Are you really fighting for money and who is going to have the furniture? Or are you just looking for another battle in your domestic war by which to hurt your spouse? If so, you will probably end up more embittered and probably substantially out of pocket as well.

### what a solicitor can do for you
A solicitor acts for one party only, and his or her professional duty is to act in that person's best long-term interests.

A solicitor should discuss your position dispassionately and advise you from the benefit of his or her experience what is likely to happen. Good advice early on may prevent matters becoming complicated or one party getting less than his or her entitlement, and can generally take the heat out of a situation. The solicitor can help you to

○ get your divorce

Divorce by the special procedure is easy enough to do without a solicitor, but where you are served with a petition and are unsure what to do about it, or your spouse flatly refuses to co-operate in any way, a solicitor would be useful.

○ sort out problems over children

Protracted litigation over the children is harmful to the children, harmful to you, and rarely produces a satisfactory result. It can also be extremely expensive. Try to reach agreement through conciliation, or suggest a meeting attended by you, your spouse and both solicitors. Disputes over children cannot be won or lost and ultimately you are likely to prefer a solution you reach together rather than one imposed upon you by a judge who, however wise and well-meaning, does not know you or your children.

○ get agreement about finances

There are cases where, whatever you do, you are faced with a long uphill battle to get financial information out of your husband or wife. However much you want to be reasonable over things, your spouse may not wish to play ball, and may refuse to disclose assets.

Withholding information at the early stages does nothing but run up costs and reduce the amount that there is to go round. If you go to see a solicitor over these problems, your spouse may then do so, too. Good solicitors will impress upon both of you the advantages of cooperation.

o get court orders for maintenance and division of property

A solicitor will know the appropriate court (magistrates' court, county court, divorce county court, High Court) for the particular order you require, and the procedure for applying.

Your resources may leave very limited room for manoeuvre and therefore there may be little point in fighting it out in court. If money disputes cannot be settled and go on for months or even years, the costs can run into thousands of pounds even where small amounts are in dispute. There is no point in getting your solicitor to try to push for more, or less, if the cost of getting it is going to be more than the amount you are asking for. Obtaining, or avoiding having to pay, the last £s of maintenance can become disproportionately expensive in terms of the extra legal costs incurred.

Even in a simple case, an hour's legal advice may be worth its weight in gold. For example, although you may have reached broad agreement over how you are going to split your finances, a solicitor may be able to

o put an agreement into wording that is clear and will be acceptable to the court
o arrange maintenance and the division of property in an efficient way from a tax point of view
o draw up a 'clean break' settlement, where appropriate
o point out things that you have not thought of: for example, that a wife may be losing substantial widow's pension rights under her husband's occupational pension scheme
o take into account the effect of any proposed order on supplementary benefit entitlement.

## how to find a solicitor

Should you decide to consult a solicitor, choose one who is experienced in matrimonial work. This may rule out the solicitor whom you have previously dealt with, perhaps about

buying the house or making your will, unless he is also
experienced in family law. That solicitor may have a partner
who specialises in divorce matters, to whom you can be
referred. But if the firm has acted for both of you in the past,
there may be a policy of acting for neither in a matrimonial
dispute. A solicitor will almost certainly not act for you if he or
she has previously acted for your husband or wife.

Ask acquaintances who have been divorced whom they
used. A recommendation can be a guide, but find out whether
the friend who was so satisfied had the same kind of problems
as you have.

The Law Society's regional directories of solicitors are available in citizens advice bureaux, public libraries and court
offices throughout the country. Each directory lists solicitors
practising in the particular area who have given information
about their availability, whether they are willing to undertake
legal aid cases and/or give fixed-fee interviews, and indicating
the categories of work they are prepared to undertake (look for
the category 'family').

*fixed-fee interview*
Some solicitors are prepared to give a 'fixed-fee' interview
under a scheme operated by the Law Society, whereby you can
get up to half-an-hour's legal advice for £5 (no extra for VAT).
This is available to everyone, irrespective of financial means.
Not all solicitors offer 'fixed-fee' interviews, so ask when
making the appointment and make it clear that you are seeing
the solicitor on that basis. Do not overstay the half hour – the
solicitor can then charge you his normal commercial rate.

**choosing the solicitor**
When you telephone or write to a firm of solicitors asking for
an appointment, say that you wish to be advised in connection
with your matrimonial difficulties, and ask if they have a
solicitor specialising in divorce and related financial matters,
perhaps one who is a member of the Solicitors Family Law
Association.

The Solicitors Family Law Association is an association of over 800 matrimonial lawyers who subscribe to a code of practice which is designed to encourage and assist parties to reach acceptable arrangements for the future in a positive and conciliatory way rather than in a litigious way. This does not mean that a SFLA solicitor will be 'soft'. His or her advice to you will be positive and so, too, should be his or her manner of dealing with the various issues that arise. You can ask the secretary of the SFLA (154 Fleet Street, London EC4A 2HX) for a list of members in your region.

### how solicitors charge

Solicitors basically charge by the hour, so that every interview, every telephone call, every letter and indeed every time the solicitor opens your file, means additional expense to you, the client. Inevitably, the longer the case goes on, the greater will be the expense.

Do not hesistate to ask what the solicitor's hourly charging (or 'charge-out') rate is, before making an appointment or at the start of the first interview. Check whether the rate includes a mark-up for 'care and attention' or whether that is additional. Remember that his charge applies not only to the time spent with you but also to writing letters, talking to witnesses or to the other spouse's solicitors, and attending court. Ask the solicitor to let you know whenever he reviews and changes his charging rate.

Value added tax is payable on solicitors' fees and there will be additional costs such as court fees, fees of any barristers engaged and, if there are major areas of dispute over the value of items of property, valuer's fees as well.

A solicitor's hourly charge may be anything from £35 to £40 plus VAT in a provincial firm, whereas in London it may be from £55 to £60 per hour plus VAT, and in really upmarket firms, charging rates of over £100 per hour plus VAT are not uncommon. So, using your solicitor as an emotional prop rather than as a legal adviser can turn out to be an extremely expensive luxury.

# Extracts from the
## Solicitors Family Law Association's
# CODE OF PRACTICE

*general*

1.1. The solicitor should endeavour to advise, negotiate and conduct proceedings in a manner calculated to encourage and assist the parties to achieve a constructive settlement of their differences as quickly as may be reasonable whilst recognising that the parties may need time to come to terms with their new situation, and should inform the client of the approach he intends to adopt.

1.2. The solicitor should treat his work in relation to the children as the most important of his duties. The solicitor should encourage the client to see the advantages to the family of a non-litigious approach as a way of resolving their disputes. The solicitor should explain to the client that in cases where there are children, the attitude of the client to the other parent in any negotiations will affect the family as a whole and may affect the relationship of the children with the parents.

1.3. The solicitor should encourage the attitude that a family dispute is not a contest in which there is one winner and one loser, but rather a search for fair solutions. He should avoid using words or phrases that imply a dispute when no serious dispute necessarily exists, for example 'opponent', 'win', 'lose', or '*Smith v Smith*' . . . . .

1.6. The solicitor should aim to avoid or dispel suspicion or mistrust between parties, by encouraging at an early stage where possible, full frank and clear disclosure of information and openness in dealings.

*relationship with client*

2.1. As a rule the solicitor should explain to the client at the outset the terms of his retainer and take care to ensure that the client is fully aware of the impact of costs on any chosen course of action. The solicitor should thereafter at all stages have regard to the cost of negotiations and proceedings . . . . .

2.3. The solicitor should create and maintain a relationship with his client of a kind which will preserve fully his independent judgement and avoid becoming so involved in the case that his own personal emotions may cloud his judgement.

2.4. Whilst recognising the need to advise firmly and guide the client the solicitor should ensure that where the decision is properly that of the client, it is taken by the client and that its consequences are fully understood, both as to its effect on any children involved and financially . . . . .

5.3. Where the purpose of taking a particular step in proceedings may be misunderstood the solicitor should consider explaining it in advance to the other party or his solicitors .

*children*

6.1. The solicitor should, in advising, negotiating and conducting proceedings, assist both his client and the other parent to regard the welfare of the child as the first and paramount consideration.

6.2. The solicitor should aim to promote cooperation between parents in decisions concerning the child, both by formal arrangements (such as orders for joint custody); by practical arrangements (such as shared involvement in school events) and by consultation on important questions . . . . .

6.5. "Kidnapping" of children both results from and creates exceptional fear, bitterness and desperation in the parents. The solicitor should therefore take what steps he properly can to prevent the kidnapping of a child and inform his client that he may be committing a criminal offence punishable by imprisonment.

The guidelines set out in this Code cannot be absolute rules in as much as the solicitor may have to depart from them if the law or his professional obligations so require. They are a restatement of principles, objectives and recommendations which many solicitors practising family law already seek to follow and to which they seek to aspire in serving their clients.

*September 1986*

Where there is dispute over custody, or maintenance and property, it is likely that both parties will have a solicitor (and perhaps barristers). There will therefore be two bills to pay at the end of the case. Whoever 'wins' or 'loses' and whoever gets an order for costs against whom, the two sets of legal fees will have to be paid out of the same source – the parties' joint assets.

In many cases, solicitors deliver interim bills 'on account' at various stages. This helps the client to know where he or she stands, and paying as the case proceeds may avoid having to find a large amount at the end.

## when seeking advice from solicitors

○ Do not hesitate to ask the solicitor to explain and discuss any points about which you are not clear.

○ Do not be embarrassed to take notes with you of what you want to ask and to take notes of the advice given.

○ Be prepared to listen to your solicitor and do not assume that cautious advice is necessarily lack of enthusiasm.

○ Remember that you can accept or reject advice as you wish. But before you reject advice make sure that you understand the point.

○ Do not leave it to your solicitor to do everything: because of the time basis of costing, the more time he or she spends on the case, the higher the bill is going to be. There is much work that can be done by you yourself that will save solicitors' costs – but tell your solicitor first what you plan to do.

○ You are entitled to be told how the case is progressing and how much it is costing at any stage. Remember to ask the solicitor for interim statements of how costs are building up.

When going to see the solicitor, take all relevant documents with you and give accurate information. Do not waste the solicitor's time by not having information ready or not listening, or by raising irrelevant points or objections just to get at your ex-partner.

It will save time if you take with you on your first appointment

○ your marriage certificate (if you can find it)
○ copies of any orders made in respect of this marriage or any previous marriage
○ a (neatly) written note setting out:
  – your names in full, and those of your spouse and children
  – dates of birth of yourself, your spouse and children
  – your address and (if different) that of your spouse
  – your home and work telephone numbers
  – your occupation and that of your spouse
  – names and addresses of the children's schools
  – dates of any previous marriage of yourself and/or your spouse
  – details of any relevant children who are not children of the marriage
  – details of any previous proceedings in respect of the marriage
  – if you have separated, the date and circumstances of the separation
○ a summary of your financial position.

Ask if you qualify for legal advice and assistance under the green form scheme, and/or for legal aid. This will depend on your financial circumstances. The limits for financial eligibility for legal advice and legal aid are reviewed by the government each year.

# the green form scheme

The basic idea behind the legal advice and assistance scheme (referred to generally in England and Wales as the 'green form scheme' because of the colour of the application form) is to allow people who would not otherwise be able to afford it to get some legal advice. You may be required to pay a contribution, depending on your income and capital.

The scheme entitles you to up to £50-worth of legal advice in the first instance (£90 if the solicitor helps to draft the divorce petition). The solicitor's hourly rate for 'green form' work is £32.50 (in London, £33.50), so you can get two or three hours' worth.

Work the solicitor may do under the green form advice and assistance scheme relevant to money and divorce includes

○ general advice on whether there are grounds for divorce or judicial separation
○ advice on questions of domicile
○ proving the validity of a foreign marriage
○ advice on the procedure for getting a divorce
○ drafting the petition and the documents to accompany it
○ advising a respondent on defending the divorce and the implications of doing so
○ help with an application for legal aid
○ advice on obtaining an injunction
○ registration of a land charge on the matrimonial home
○ advice about custody, care and control of children, and access
○ advice about maintenance, and arrangements concerning the matrimonial home
○ correspondence or discussions with solicitors acting for the other spouse to try to negotiate a settlement.

One green form covers all matters 'arising from proceedings for divorce or judicial separation'. This means that the applicant is not entitled to £50-worth (or £90-worth, as the case may be) of green form assistance for each matter connected with the divorce – the divorce itself, maintenance, custody and injunctions. There is only one green form for all that. If, however, there are other matters, such as housing or supplementary benefit, hire purchase debts, or whatever, each of those can form the subject of a separate green form application and entitle the person to, in the first instance, £50-worth of advice.

A separate green form could cover

o correspondence with building societies, hire purchase and finance companies and public utilities with regard to problems about payment of bills, instalments or other debts following the breakdown of a marriage
o advice on entitlement to social security benefits and other welfare rights
o drawing up a new will.

The one thing a solicitor cannot do under the green form scheme is actually to conduct the case on your behalf, or to appear for you in the divorce court. However, for a hearing in the magistrates' court (in connection with maintenance or a protection or exclusion order perhaps), the solicitor can apply to the legal aid area office for approval to represent his client in that court.

The green form scheme is appropriate for simple undefended divorces or for negotiating straightforward settlements. When the initial limit of £50 or £90 is used up, the solicitor can apply to the Law Society's legal aid area office to extend the limit. One request for an extension is usually granted.

## eligibility for the green form scheme

Eligibility for the green form scheme is based on financial limits.

The solicitor carries out the assessment of your financial means while you are with him, based on the figures provided by you. The solicitor will ask about your savings and other capital and about your gross weekly income, your outgoings and any dependants. He enters these details on the green form, and can tell you straightaway whether you are eligible for the legal advice scheme.

The figures given here came into effect in April 1987.

*capital*
Your disposable capital must not exceed £825, or £1,025 if you have one dependant, £1,145 if two dependants, increasing by £60 for each additional dependant. The value of your home and its contents, personal clothing and tools of a trade are not counted as part of disposable capital.

Anyone receiving supplementary benefit or family income supplement is automatically eligible for the green form scheme, subject to the disposable capital threshold. So, someone getting supplementary benefit but who has savings of, say, £2,500 would not be eligible for the green form scheme.

☆ From April 1988, supplementary benefit is to be replaced by 'income support' and family income supplement by 'family credit'.

*income*
The disposable income limit is £118 in the last seven days.

Disposable income is your weekly income after deduction of tax and national insurance contributions and after deducting an allowance for any dependants, namely:

£29.70 for a spouse
£13.00 for a child under 11
£19.50 for a child aged 11 to 15
£23.45 for a child aged 16 or 17
£30.45 for a dependant aged 18 or over.

The income of the spouse is not included where husband and wife have a contrary interest in the case at issue. This means that often the non-working wife of even a very wealthy man is eligible for the green form scheme.

**contribution**

If your disposable income is £56 or less per week, you will not be required to pay any contribution but if it is between £56 and £118, a contribution will be required from you. This is a single payment, on a scale from £5 up to £64.

It is probably worthwhile to get advice under the green form scheme even if you have to pay a high contribution because the cost of legal advice will undoubtedly be more if you pay privately, and under the green form scheme you will be exempt from some court fees.

If you are eligible, you will have to sign the green form, confirming that the information given is correct and that you accept the terms of the scheme. If your disposable income is high enough for you to have to pay a contribution, you will be asked to pay the appropriate amount to the solicitor straight-away (but you may be allowed to pay in instalments).

# the legal aid scheme

Where there is likely to be any contest, or a hearing in court, the green form scheme would not be adequate but you can apply for a legal aid certificate.

Under the legal aid scheme, which is funded by the state and administered by the Law Society, an eligible applicant gets the services of a solicitor (and barrister, where appropriate) free, or on payment of an assessed contribution towards the cost.

Legal aid is available for applications in a divorce court relating to any maintenance orders, property orders, lump sum orders and contested arrangements for children. Legal aid is not normally available for an undefended divorce by the special procedure.

The solicitor can supply the application form for legal aid. The form requires details of the applicant, his wife or her husband and children, and a summary of the applicant's case. It is not all that straightforward to complete; the solicitor will help you with the form, but he can charge you for this (unless you are eligible for advice under the green form scheme).

The application is sent to the secretary of the legal aid area office for consideration of the legal merits of your case and to the legal aid assessment officer of the Department of Health and Social Security to assess what contribution is required. You will be sent a 12-page financial statement form to complete. On this you will have to give full details of yourself; your home; your regular income from investments and work; your valuables and savings. There is also a form for your employer to complete. For self-employed people, there is a different financial statement form.

## financial eligibility for legal aid

As with the green form scheme, the criteria are disposable income and the amount of disposable capital. If either is above the limit, you are ineligible for legal aid.

In a matrimonial dispute, the spouse's income or capital can be ignored for all calculations of disposable income and disposable capital.

The figures given here came into effect in April 1987.

### income

Disposable income is your annual income net of tax and national insurance contributions, but including child benefit and any maintenance (net of tax) received under a court order or agreement from your spouse. From this will be deducted

○ expenses incurred in connection with employment such as fares to work, trade union membership dues, child-minding costs
○ rent, or mortgage repayments
○ rates
○ HP commitments

○ insurance commitments
○ maintenance paid to spouse from whom you are living apart
○ allowance for dependants: if you and your spouse are living together, £1,544 is deducted from annual income for wife, and £676 to £1,583 for each dependant, according to age.

A contribution towards your costs will be required unless your disposable income is less than £2,325. The most you can be asked to pay by way of contribution is one-quarter of the amount (25p for every £) by which your disposable income is above £2,325 and under £5,585, up to a maximum of £815.

| *disposable income* | |
|---|---|
| if under £2,325 a year | 'free' legal aid i.e. no contribution (provided capital also within 'free' limit) |
| if between £2,325 and £5,585 | contribution required (25% of excess over £2,325) |
| £5,585 | upper limit for legal aid |

**capital**
For disposable capital, ignored are

○ value of the house you live in
○ value of any other property or money that is in dispute between you and your spouse
○ furniture, personal clothing, tools of trade, car.

Apart from this, virtually everything that is capable of being valued in money terms will count as disposable capital: not merely cash or deposits or shares but sums that could be borrowed on the security of insurance policies. Also counted in are furs and jewellery (other than engagement ring or wedding ring), antiques and other valuables.

Where the capital assets come to between £3,000 and £4,850 you will have to contribute a lump sum equal to the capital above £3,000 (this means a maximum of £1,850). This payment is additional to any contribution that has to be made because of your income.

*disposable capital*

| | |
|---|---|
| if under £3,000 | 'free' legal aid i.e. no contribution (provided income also within 'free' limit) |
| if between £3,000 and £4,850 | contribution required (on excess over £3,000) |
| £4,850 | upper limit for legal aid |

**waiting for the decision**
You have to wait some weeks before knowing whether a legal aid certificate will be issued; the waiting time may run into several months. A legal aid certificate cannot cover work done before the date the certificate is issued. By now, the costs limit of the green form scheme is likely to have been reached, and the Law Society is unlikely to allow any further extensions on a green form, so effectively this means that your case will come to a halt once an application for legal aid has been made, unless you are prepared and able to pay the solicitor yourself.

*emergency legal aid*
In cases of real emergency (for example, an application for an injunction), an interim legal aid certificate can be granted almost immediately. You have to fill in a special pink form

(which the solicitor will provide) explaining why the application is urgent.

If it is granted, you must then apply for and provide all the details for getting a full legal aid certificate (even if you do not want to take the case any further). If you do not, you will yourself have to meet the costs incurred under the emergency certificate.

### the offer and contributions

If the decision is that you are eligible and no contribution is required, a legal aid certificate is sent to you and to your solicitor.

If a contribution is required, you are sent an offer setting out details of the amount required and how you will be expected to pay it. Contributions based on income normally have to be paid by 12 monthly instalments; the capital sum there and then. Initially, the contribution on your capital will not be for more than the expected cost of your case. If the contribution you are asked to make seems to be unreasonably high in relation to the likely cost of your case, you can ask for a reassessment.

The legal aid certificate will not be issued until after you have accepted the offer and made the first of the monthly contributions and any lump sum payment. It is important to keep up monthly payments and to carry out the conditions of the legal aid certificate (such as informing the legal aid office of any changes in your financial situation, perhaps because of maintenance payments). If you do not, you run the risk of your certificate being withdrawn and finding yourself liable for your legal costs.

No work done by the solicitor before the legal aid certificate was issued is covered. The solicitor is entitled to charge you for any pre-certificate work and you will have to pay (unless the work was carried out under the green form scheme).

Once a legal aid certificate is granted, the solicitor must act in every way as for a fee-paying client.

### *if your income or capital changes*

If your disposable income increases by more than £500 per annum, or decreases by more than £250 per annum in the twelve months following the assessment, you must inform the Law Society via your solicitor (for example, if a maintenance order is made while property and custody matters are still being contested).

You will be reassessed and your contribution may be adjusted or the certificate 'discharged' (that is, ended) so that you become responsible for your legal costs from then on.

If there is an increase in income later than twelve months after the first assessment, the Law Society can order a reassessment only with a view to discharging a certificate, not to change the contribution required.

As far as disposable capital is concerned, you are supposed to report increases of £120 or more. You may be called upon to pay another lump sum contribution or the certificate may be taken away if you are now over the capital limit.

### *legal fees when on legal aid*

When a person is granted legal aid, he or she ceases to become personally responsible for his or her own legal fees. The solicitor should not bill the client direct for work within the limits of the legal aid certificate. Fees of solicitors and barristers and any other disbursements during the existence of the certificate, will be paid by the Law Society.

Many people think that because they are legally aided, they are not going to pay anything. But they may be required to contribute to the cost of those fees, not only by paying a contribution as a condition of receiving legal aid but by being required to make good any shortfall on the legal aid fund out of any property recovered or preserved in the proceedings. This is the statutory legal aid charge or 'first charge'.

---

☆ The whole of the legal aid system is at present under discussion and considerable changes are proposed in the 1987 Legal Aid Bill being presented to Parliament.

## the statutory charge

The statutory charge is intended to recoup some of the tax-payer's money which finances the legal aid fund.

When the legal aid fund has to pay out more than it collects by way of contribution from the 'assisted' (that is, the legally-aided) person and from any costs the other side is ordered to pay, it then has a first charge on any property which has been in issue in the proceedings and which has been recovered, or preserved under the terms of a compromise to avoid or bring an end to proceedings.

'In the proceedings' means all proceedings in the same suit or action for which legal aid was granted, not just those relating to the property recovered or preserved. For example, if the legal aid certificate covered the divorce, a custody application, an injunction and a transfer of property order application, the cost of all those proceedings would be part of the charge on the property transferred.

In matrimonial proceedings, the first £2,500 of any property gained or preserved is exempt from the statutory charge, and the charge does not apply to any maintenance payments.

Solicitors should hand to all applicants for legal aid a leaflet explaining how the scheme works and should also personally explain to a particular applicant how the statutory charge may affect her or him. The Law Society has produced a booklet, *Understanding the statutory charge*, mainly intended for lawyers, available free from legal aid area offices and from the legal aid head office: Newspaper House, 8–16 Great New Street, London EC4A 3BN.

### on property

Property could be a lump sum payment, the value of the house (or a share of it) and any other asset that was transferred or handed over or has been kept.

Property is held to have been recovered or preserved if it has been in issue in the proceedings – that is, it has been the subject of an application – even if the case is settled halfway through without an order having been made or an order is made based on agreement.

Only if the property was genuinely never in dispute would there be no risk of the statutory charge applying in the end. For example, if you came to a final agreement before the application for legal aid or if in correspondence it had been conceded that the other party always had the property rather than that it was now being transferred, this would be evidence that there was no element of dispute. Ideally, if it could be achieved in time, send an agreed statement with the application for legal aid, so that the Law Society would know from the start that there was no property that would be gained or preserved through the proceedings.

### *postponement and substitution*
Where the property is a house and is being transferred rather than sold, the legally aided person to whom it has been transferred does not have to pay the statutory charge there and then. Instead, the charge is put on the house and is not enforced until the house is sold. No interest is payable.

The legal aid fund's postponement of enforcing the charge is relevant also when property has been preserved. For example, if the house belongs to the wife and the husband's application for a share in it does not succeed, the wife has preserved her ownership of the house and the statutory charge will be enforced, but only when she comes to sell the house.

When the house is being sold so that another one can be bought with the proceeds of sale, the legal aid fund may agree to put the charge on the substitute dwelling house, provided that

○ the net value of the new home covers the amount of the charge
  *and*

○ it is to be the sole residence of the assisted person and at least one unmarried child under 18 or in full-time education at the

date of purchase of the substitute home, or it is necessary for the assisted person or his or her dependants to move for reasons of health, disability or employment
*and*
○ the substitution is just and reasonable and a refusal would cause hardship to the assisted person.

Only in exceptional cases will substitution be allowed more than once.

The charge on property other than the home – for instance, a lump sum – can never be postponed. This would include a lump sum that arises out of the sale of a house or one intended for the purchase of a home.

### examples of legal aid and the statutory charge
The following fictitious and real-life examples show how the legal aid charge 'bites', sometimes in unexpected circumstances.

*example 1*
The wife applies for legal aid, which is granted with no contribution required. The couple's marriage has lasted over ten years and there are two children. They live in their own house which, after deducting the outstanding mortgage debt, is now worth £20,000.

The house was bought in the husband's name. The wife has worked throughout the marriage and has helped with the mortgage payments, so that it can be argued that she has a right to a share in the value of the house. She applies for a transfer of the whole house to herself; he applies for a transfer of her share to him. On the basis that she is prepared to forgo maintenance, the court orders that he should transfer the whole house to her.

The result of this is that the whole of the property has been in issue; she has 'recovered' her husband's share and 'preserved' whatever undefined share she had. Therefore, the statutory charge can be up to the full net value of the house (£20,000), minus the £2,500 which is exempt.

Unless she gets an order for costs against the husband, she will be liable to repay the legal aid fund for her full legal costs: not just the costs of the property transfer application but also those of any other proceedings which may have been taken under the certificate – such as a custody application – irrespective of the fact that she has not received any money out of which to meet the charge. However, she will not be required to pay straightaway: the legal aid fund postpones payment of the charge until the house is sold.

### example 2
*(based on the case of Simmons v Simmons)*
The wife, who was legally aided, was still living in the matrimonial home, the net value of which was £38,500. After protracted proceedings, having run up £8,000 of legal costs, an order was made for the house to be sold and out of the proceeds the wife to receive a lump sum of £26,750. It was a sum carefully arrived at to enable the wife to buy another home for herself and the children, with the aid of a further sum she could raise on mortgage. Apparently it did not occur to anybody at first that she would not get £26,750 at all, but only £18,750, because the legal aid charge would 'bite' as soon as the matrimonial home was sold and the lump sum paid to her. The legal aid fund has no discretion to postpone the enforcement of a charge against cash.

(A practice direction has since been issued by the Divorce Registry requiring solicitors of legally aided clients to provide an estimate of their costs at the hearing so that the court can take account of the effect of the statutory charge.)

The moral is always to seek clear legal advice about the way in which the legal aid charge may affect any possible solution to property disputes.

*example 3*
*(based on the case of Hanlon v The Law Society)*
The wife was granted a legal aid certificate. The former matrimonial home was in the husband's sole name but it was argued that she had a right to a share by virture of having contributed to the mortgage payments. She applied for and got an order that the home be transferred to her outright. He had initially defended the divorce, and applied for an order that such interest as she might have in the house be transferred to him. Therefore, the whole of the matrimonial home was 'in issue'.

During the course of the protracted proceedings, her costs ran up to over £8,000, made up as follows:

| | |
|---|---:|
| divorce and injunction applications | £925 |
| custody proceedings | £1,150 |
| applications for maintenance and property adjustment orders | £5,950 |
| | £8,025 |

The legal aid fund had a charge on all of the £8,025. The net value of the matrimonial home was at that time only £10,000, so all that the wife would get if the house were sold would be £2,500 (the exemption), the other £7,500 going towards the £8,025 charge. The husband was legally aided throughout but, because he neither preserved nor gained anything, the legal aid fund paid all his legal costs (except for the amount of the contribution he was required to make).

The real problem did not arise until the wife wanted to sell the house because it was proving too expensive to run. The legal aid fund did not (and still does not) enforce the charge on a matrimonial home when it is recovered by the legally-aided party until the property comes to be sold. The House of Lords held that she could sell the house and use the money for buying a new house.

She did not have to pay the statutory charge then but the legal aid fund took a substitute charge on the new property she bought.

*example 4*
*(based on Curling v The Law Society)*
The husband and wife were divorcing on the grounds of her adultery. They had agreed throughout that each was entitled to half the net equity of their house. The husband wanted to stay there with the children, deferring the sale. He applied in his petition for custody of the children and a property adjustment order. He then applied for an ouster injunction to exclude her from the home; this was due for hearing on the same day as the custody proceedings. The wife was legally aided.

Before the hearing, the husband gave up his claim for custody and agreed to pay his wife £15,000 in return for her half of the net equity, valued at £30,900. A consent order was made for the lump sum.

It was held that the statutory charge applied to the lump sum received by the wife. Even though the ownership of the house had never been in dispute, the wife's right to recover the property had been in issue because her share had been locked away from her by the husband's insistence on staying in possession. She therefore had to pay back to the legal aid fund the legal costs for her part in all the proceedings out of the sum she received for her share of the house.

*example 5*
Husband and wife and two children live in a council house. He walks out on the wife and pays her no maintenance. The wife, who does not work, claims supplementary benefit. The husband admits adultery, and asks for a divorce.

The wife goes to a solicitor for advice under the green form scheme (no contribution is required from her because she is on supplementary benefit) for help with her divorce petition and also advice on transferring the tenancy wholly to her.

The husband becomes violent towards the wife and the children, and she has to apply for an injunction. He claims custody and causes difficulty over agreeing about access.

For all of these matters, the wife gets legal aid (no contribution required). However many hundreds of pounds are run up in legal fees on her behalf, she will never have to pay a penny to the legal aid fund, because no property on which any value can be placed has been 'recovered or preserved'. The local authority tenancy has no value in this context.

The husband applies for legal aid to defend the transfer of property application and the injunction and to apply for custody. He gets a legal aid certificate subject to a contribution. Win or lose, however, he will not be required to pay anything more towards his own legal costs.

The net result is that the legal aid fund ends up paying virtually the whole of both parties' costs.

### legal aid costs
High legal costs can be run up over what may in essence be quite trivial disputes. Solicitors' duty to the legal aid fund requires them to report to the Law Society if they consider that the client is asking for litigation unreasonably – for example, by refusing to accept an offer of settlement.

Even though you are on legal aid, it is important to ask your solicitor to keep you posted on the costs of the case, particularly where the house or a lump sum is being negotiated for, and to explain to you what the statutory charge may entail in your case.

### *paying the charge*
In legally aided cases, any lump sum payment ordered by the court has to be paid to the solicitor: only he can give a receipt for it. He has to pay it all into the legal aid fund, but if he undertakes that the cost of the case will not be more than £xxx, he can pay just that amount into the fund and the rest direct to the recipient. Otherwise, the recipient has to wait until the legal aid fund has settled up the costs before being paid the balance.

# legal advice and/or legal aid

| | 'green form' scheme (legal advice and assistance) | legal aid scheme |
|---|---|---|
| who is eligible? | anyone with disposable income not more than £118 p.w.† and with disposable capital not more than £825‡ | anyone with disposable income not more than £5,585 p.a.† and with disposable capital not more than £4,850‡ |
| what does it cover? | advice, and help with documents up to £50-worth (@ hourly rate of £32.50) or £90-worth if solicitor drafts divorce petition | all legal work required including representation in court by solicitor and, if necessary, barrister |
| how long does it go on for? | until cost limit reached (but can apply for extension) | until case concluded |
| how does one apply? | by giving information to solicitor about income and savings; he completes 'green form' if eligible | by giving information to solicitor to complete application form to pass on to area legal aid office with details of grounds for case, and to DHSS assessment office with details of income, expenses and capital |

| | | |
|---|---|---|
| **how long does decision take?** | solicitor decides there and then | weeks or months while assessment being made; solicitor will not start legal aid work until certificate issued (emergency certificate may be granted in urgent case) |
| **what does it cost me?** | if disposable income between £56 and £118 p.w., contribution (from £5 to £64) payable there and then; can be paid in instalments where lump sum over £2500 gained, solicitor's charge taken from it | if disposable income between £2,325 and £5,585 p.a., contribution payable by monthly instalments and if disposable capital between £3,000 and £4,850, contribution payable when offer of legal aid is accepted on gain or preservation of property over £2500 where statutory charge arises, remaining legal costs of case taken from property recovered or preserved |
| | † contribution required if more than £56 p.w. ‡ higher if dependants | † contribution required if more than £2,325 p.a. ‡ contribution required if more than £3,000 |

# GETTING MONEY BEFORE A DIVORCE

If you are not at the stage of petitioning for divorce or judicial separation, you can apply to the local magistrates' court or the county court for an order for financial provision from your spouse if he or she is not providing proper maintenance for you or the children. Getting a court order may be useful even if you can agree interim financial arrangements (in which case, you can ask for an order to be made in your agreed terms – a 'consent order'). An order is generally easier to enforce than a simple separation agreement and is the only route to tax efficiency in respect of payments to children.

## through the county court

An application can be made to any county court for maintenance or a lump sum payment, even when no divorce is required or possible. You have to satisfy the court that your spouse has failed to provide reasonable maintenance for you or for any child of the family.

An affidavit in support has to be submitted with details of the applicant's financial resources and needs. The respondent is required to file an affidavit in answer within 14 days of the service of the application upon him or her by the court. The county court registrar normally hears the application in chambers in the same way as an application for maintenance in divorce proceedings.

It is unlikely that you will be able to get a legal aid certificate for an application to the county court; the Law Society's *Notes for guidance* in the *Legal Aid handbook* said that 'Where the magistrates' court is able to provide the relief the client is seeking . . . legal advisers will normally be expected to commence proceedings in the magistrates' court'.

## through the magistrates' court

The magistrates' court can make orders for periodical payments for any amount and for lump sums of up to £500 each for the applicant and any children. The lump sum can be, for example, to repay the applicant for expenses reasonably incurred in maintaining herself or himself and the children during the period before the order was made.

You have to be able to prove that your spouse

o has deserted you, or
o has behaved in such a way that you cannot reasonably be expected to live with him or her (this could include adultery by your spouse), or
o has failed to provide reasonable maintenance for you or the children.

If you and your spouse have agreed about maintenance, you can go to the magistrates' court and ask for an agreed order to be made along those lines provided the court has no reason to think it would be unjust. (There is no upper limit on lump sums in 'agreed' orders.) If the order contains provision for a child, the court has a specific duty to check that a proper contribution is being made towards the child's needs.

Being able to get an order in the magistrates' court is particularly useful where you do not propose to divorce in the immediate future but want a court order for maintenance for tax reasons – especially for children's maintenance.

### *applying*
The procedure for applying for a maintenance order in a magistrates' court is simple and costs relatively little; no affidavits are required. The application can be made to any

magistrates' court in the area where either husband or wife lives, or where they last lived together. Legal aid (or approval for 'assistance by way of representation' under the green form scheme) can be applied for to make or defend such an application.

Both the applicant and the respondent will be asked to provide evidence about their income and expenditure and assets. Before making any order, the magistrates' court takes into account all the circumstances of the case, giving first consideration to the welfare of any child of the family. Other factors are income and earning capacities, obligations and responsibilities, age, any physical disabilities, duration of the marriage, previous standard of living, the contribution each has made to the family and the conduct of each of the parties if it would be unfair not to take it into account.

The interval between applying to the magistrates' court and the hearing varies from court to court; it is likely to be between one and two months. In a case of urgent need, a court can be asked for an expedited hearing, or an interim order to tide the applicant over until such time as the case can be heard fully. An interim maintenance order lasts for a maximum of 3 months and may be extended for three months more. (But the Inland Revenue may not allow tax relief on interim payments.)

If subsequently there is a petition for divorce, details of any magistrates' court order for maintenance have to be given on it, where information is asked about 'other proceedings in any court'.

An order made by a magistrates' court can be discharged by the divorce court when making orders as to maintenance or for a lump sum or property adjustment.

## through the divorce court

Once the petition has been lodged at the divorce county court, an application for an order for financial provision can be made there. If you have obtained an order for maintenance at the magistrates' court or county court, this remains in force until there is an order in the divorce county court.

## maintenance pending suit

None of the long-term orders for maintenance can be made until the decree nisi and do not take effect until the decree has been made absolute. However, the court has power to order temporary maintenance payments for a spouse until the decree absolute. This is known as maintenance 'pending suit'. The main point of the m.p.s. order is to keep the wife and children going until an order can be made after fuller examination of the overall financial position. Interim payments orders may similarly be made for any children.

An application for maintenance pending suit and for children's interim periodical payments can be made as soon as the petition is filed. It may take 3 to 6 weeks for the application to be heard. You will have to give the fullest possible information about your needs and provide an affidavit of means, as should the respondent. If the respondent fails to file an affidavit of means, the registrar may make the order for quite a high amount in order to bring the respondent's financial affairs into the open – he must pay up, or disclose his finances if he wants to prove that the order is too high for him to manage.

Maintenance pending suit is in the nature of an interim order until the court has had an opportunity to consider fully the claim for financial provision. It comes into effect straight-away but may be backdated to the date of the petition, and lasts at most until decree absolute. As its purpose is to tide you over until there can be a full inquiry into all the financial facts, this is generally reflected in the level of payment ordered.

## separation agreements

If you and your spouse can agree financial arrangements following separation and there is no tax advantage to be gained by way of court orders providing for children, you might like simply to record the terms you have agreed. But you cannot write into the agreement that neither party has the right to invoke the subsequent assistance of the courts.

Provided the terms are intended to be enforceable, they should result in maintenance payments by one spouse to another qualifying for tax relief, just as if the payments were due under a court order.

Although a separation agreement can seem quite informal, it can have profound repercussions in the form of tax consequences, enforceability and – if it just deals with interim maintenance – by generally paving the way for future long-term financial arrangements.

If the agreement deals not just with interim maintenance but is intended to resolve all financial matters once and for all, and one spouse subsequently changes his or her mind and asks the court to review the position, the court may well hold both parties to the terms they had agreed. The court is particularly likely to uphold the original terms if both spouses had received independent legal advice and there had been full financial disclosure. It is wise, therefore, to consult a solicitor to check the terms you or your spouse have in mind and perhaps to draft the appropriate documentation. And, in any event, do not fail to send a copy of the agreement to your inspector of taxes.

## from the state

When the marriage breaks up and you have separated, you may find that you need – and now qualify for – financial help from the state.

Most generally applicable is supplementary benefit for someone not in full-time work and family income supplement for someone who is in work and has at least one child.

☆ Current government proposals for replacing supplementary benefit with an income support scheme, and family income supplement with a family credit scheme, are due to take effect from April 1988. ☆

Both supplementary benefit (SB) and family income supplement (FIS) are a 'passport' to various other benefits, such as free dental treatment, free milk and vitamins for a child under 5, school meals without charge, and legal advice and assistance under the green form scheme and exemption from some court fees.

For either supplementary benefit or FIS, you have to apply to the DHSS (Department of Health and Social Security) on the appropriate forms, available from post offices, social security offices and citizens advice bureaux. The DHSS leaflet FB27, *Bringing up children?*, includes information for one-parent families, and leaflet FB2 *Which benefit?* tells you how to work out your entitlement to supplementary benefit and family income supplement.

### supplementary benefit

Full-time work for supplementary benefit purposes is 30 hours a week: if you work longer, you do not qualify. Someone without a job normally has to register as available for work. But a lone parent with a child under 16 living with him or her can claim supplementary benefit without registering for work.

You are not eligible for supplementary benefit if your capital or savings are more than £3,000 (but certain types of capital may be fully or partially ignored). For income, there is not one single threshold figure: it is based on the scale rate applying to the category of your personal status – married couple, single person, children according to age. The scale rate is meant to meet normal day-to-day living expenses (except housing costs); any additional requirements are taken into account for individual cases. The scale rate figures are revised by the government each year.

The DHSS calculate supplementary benefit by making a list of all the requirements a household has, and taking away the resources coming in. If your resources fall short of the scale rate requirements, supplementary benefit is payable to bring you up to your appropriate scale rate. After 52 weeks of receiving supplementary benefit without being required to be available for work, the 'long-term' rate, which is considerably higher, comes into effect.

Your 'resources' are all the money you have coming in, such as child benefit and any earnings. Earnings are taken net, and allowance is made for such expenses as fares for getting to work and cost of child-minding. The first £4 a week of net earnings are disregarded and for single parents only half of any net earnings between £4 and £20 a week is taken into account. So, a single parent can earn £20 net a week and have only £8 deducted from her or his entitlement to supplementary benefit.

Single payments for exceptional needs can also be requested by someone receiving supplementary benefit, but if you have capital over £500, you would be expected to use the excess before such a payment could be made. There are other fairly stringent provisions. A citizens advice bureau can be asked for advice on this.

A claim form for supplementary benefit is in the DHSS leaflet SB1. The *Supplementary Benefits Handbook* is a guide to claimants' rights, published by HMSO (1984 edition, £2.50). The Child Poverty Action Group's *National Welfare Benefits Handbook* gives detailed information and advice (1987 edition £4.50 from 1-5 Bath Street, London EC1V 9PY). DHSS leaflet SB16 describes extra payments for people on supplementary benefit, leaflet SB18 explains the capital rule, and leaflet SB19 deals with weekly payments for special needs.

*supplementary benefit and court orders*
Sometimes a court order is made for maintenance which just takes the wife out of her existing supplementary benefit entitlement. This means that she would lose her right to free school meals for the children and so on, and she would also lose the right to any special needs payments. Also, an order just taking the wife off supplementary benefit while she is still on the lower rate will do her out of the higher long-term rate which she would have become entitled to after 12 months on benefit. This can be a real hardship to the wife – and often to the husband who may have been ordered to pay a bit more to his wife whereas, in fact, she receives less.

If a lump sum is ordered by the court, the amount may bring her above the capital limit and supplementary benefit would then cease, or the income which is assumed by the DHSS to derive from the lump sum may make her no longer eligible.

If a woman has to claim supplementary benefit because the husband is not paying the maintenance he was ordered to pay and he eventually pays off the arrears, she will be asked to repay any supplementary benefit payments she had been receiving in the meantime.

*children*
After divorce, a man remains legally responsible for maintaining his children. If he does not do so and the mother has to claim supplementary benefit for them, the DHSS will try to get the man (if he can be located) to pay the amount they are giving out to the mother by way of benefit for the children. If he refuses, they can take him to court. (Although the man may be able to afford to pay more, he cannot be forced to do so by the DHSS. Moreover, every £1 he pays above the supplementary benefit figures for the children will be deducted, £ for £, from the mother's supplementary benefit payment.)

**housing benefit**
Help with rent and/or rates is provided through the housing benefit scheme. Most supplementary benefit recipients qualify for 100 per cent housing benefit. However, if there are non-

dependants, such as lodgers or grown-up children, living in the household, or in the case of tenants paying rent, if this includes a charge for heating, there may be some rent and/or rates still payable.

☆ Current government proposals to introduce changes in assessment and criteria for housing benefit as part of the income support scheme are due to come into effect in April 1988. ☆

the DHSS automatically notifies the local authority when someone comes on to supplementary benefit, and then the local council

○ **for an owner-occupier** credits the person's rates account with the amount of benefit payable (i.e. the rates are 'paid' either in full or in part by a paper transaction).
○ **for a council tenant** credits the person's rent and rates account with the amount due (another paper transaction). The tenant may still have to pay something – for example, if a charge for heating is payable with the rent, he may have to pay that out of his weekly supplementary benefit payment.
○ **for a private tenant** the council credits the rates account (if they are not paid separately), and sends the tenant a cheque for the amount of his rent (in certain circumstances, it can be paid directly to the landlord).

Someone who is not eligible for supplementary benefit may still qualify for housing benefit. The amount of help depends on the person's income, size of family, amount of rent and rates payable and whether there are non-dependants living in the household. She or he may also qualify for a special payment to help with remaining housing costs – this is called housing benefit supplement. The local DHSS office can be asked for more information about this.

SHAC (London Housing Aid Centre, 189a Old Brompton Road, London SW5 0AR) has three leaflets about housing benefit: one for council tenants, one for home owners and one for private and housing association tenants. The leaflets cost 25p each.

**family income supplement**
FIS is a weekly cash payment for a family on low wages with one or more dependent children under 16 (or still at school and under 19). Unlike supplementary benefit where you are not eligible if you work more than a certain number of hours a week, FIS is paid only if you work at least so-many hours each week. When a couple have separated, either parent can claim, provided she or he works not less than 24 hours a week and the children are living with her or him. There is therefore an overlap between supplementary benefit and FIS.

DHSS leaflet FIS 1 includes a claim form and gives details of conditions and rates.

The amount of the supplement is one-half of the difference between the parent's gross income and the appropriate FIS level for the size of the family, subject to a prescribed maximum. Certain items of income are disregarded, such as child benefit, gifts from relatives, payments in kind. A lump sum awarded as part of financial provision on marriage breakdown would be disregarded, but interest from savings or capital is taken into account when assessing entitlement to FIS.

Family income supplement is tax-free. Once the parent is eligible, the payment is made for a whole year, even if financial circumstances change. This may mean that an increase in the mother's income through maintenance payments during the currency of the FIS award would not affect the amount of FIS being paid to her. And it may be possible for the registrar to give the husband a few months' breathing space by ordering lower maintenance payments until just before the current FIS assessment runs out and, in the order, provide for an increase at that time. The order would be, for example, for £8 per month for 5 months and £30 per month thereafter.

*FIS or SB?*
It is possible to be a full-time worker for FIS purposes (24 hours a week if a single parent) and part-time for supplementary benefit purposes (less than 30 hours a week).

Single parents who work between 24 and 30 hours a week

face a tricky calculation: are they better off claiming FIS or SB? You can go to a citizens advice bureau and ask for help with working out the answer in your particular circumstances.

### child benefit
Where a married couple are living together, child benefit is normally paid to the wife. But if the couple separate or divorce, child benefit will be paid to the parent (either one or both) with whom the children are living.

You should report your separation or divorce to your local social security office if you are getting child benefit, or if you have not been getting it yet but now have one or more of your children living with you. The claim form is CH2.

Child benefit is treated as a resource when supplementary benefit entitlement is calculated.

### *one-parent benefit*
One-parent benefit is an additional payment to a separated or divorced parent who is getting child benefit. The amount is the same regardless of the number of children. One-parent benefit is not payable when the parent is on supplementary benefit.

You can claim after you have been living apart from your spouse for 13 weeks, or from the date of your divorce or legal separation if this is sooner than the 13 weeks. But it is not paid if you start living with someone as husband and wife.

# THE HOME BEFORE A DIVORCE

A spouse who does not legally own the home – that is, whose name is not on the title deeds – has certain rights of occupation:

○ the right not to be evicted without a court order if he or she is in occupation
○ the right (if the court thinks fit) to return to the home if he or she has left it
○ the right (if the court thinks fit) to exclude the owner spouse from occupying the home for a period.

The same occupation rights apply if the home is rented.

These are short-term rights of occupation while the marriage is still in being. The long-term decisions about the rights to live in the home or to get a share of the proceeds if sold will have to be made as part of the divorce settlement.

These rights can be protected by an order in the magistrates' court or an injunction in the county court.

### in the magistrates' court
The magistrates' court can be asked for a personal protection order to restrain a spouse who has used or threatened violence towards the other spouse and/or children. Where there is imminent danger of physical injury, an expedited order can be made; most courts will arrange an emergency hearing the same day as the application.

Where violence has been used towards the other spouse or a child, or violence threatened to that spouse or child or used towards any other person, the magistrates' court can be asked for an exclusion order. This orders the violent spouse to leave the home or, if he or she has already left, not to return. In cases of actual physical injury to the applicant or a child, the court may attach a power of arrest to the order, so that the offending spouse can be arrested without a warrant and brought before a magistrate.

Where a person is receiving legal advice under the green form scheme, an application can be made to the legal aid area office for approval of 'assistance by way of representation' (known as ABWOR) which, if granted, covers a solicitor's representing his client in the magistrates' court for an application for an exclusion order or a protection order.

### getting an injunction
The realities of life are that one spouse may try to force the other to leave, by violent means or other pressure. Where there is actual or feared violence, or behaviour that may cause harm, it may be possible to obtain a court order against the threatening spouse, requiring him or her to leave, or not to return to the home, or not to come within a specified area, or to confine himself or herself to a defined part of the home, or not to assault, molest or in any way interfere with the other spouse and/or children. Molestation can include pestering such as repeated telephone calls or other forms of harassment.

The two forms of injunction are commonly referred to as an 'ouster' injunction and a 'non-molestation' injunction.

The application for an injunction can be made to the county court, whether or not divorce proceedings have started or are envisaged. Where divorce proceedings have started, 'ouster' proceedings can be brought in the same county court as the one where the divorce is being sought.

The cost of obtaining an injunction is likely to be some hundreds of pounds, and injunction proceedings should be considered carefully before being commenced. You should get a solicitor's advice on an application for an injunction. (The green form scheme allows for this.) Similarly, if an injunction is served on you, you should get legal advice.

Legal aid is available for an injunction and it is possible for an emergency legal aid certificate to be granted immediately.

*applying for an injunction*
An application for an injunction has to be supported by an affidavit giving particulars of any children, of the accommodation and alternative accommodation available to each party, and of the conduct complained of, and why an injunction is necessary.

The other spouse should produce an affidavit dealing with the allegations and can suggest solutions, such as alternative accommodation or the possibility of remaining living in the same house.

An emergency application for an injunction can be heard very quickly – usually in a few days or, in a real emergency, straightaway even without written affidavit evidence.

In 'ex parte' proceedings, where the other spouse is not given advance notice of the hearing, he or she will be given the opportunity to put his or her case before the court at a resumed hearing, usually about one week later. A non-molestation injunction may be made 'ex parte' if the situation seems very serious, but for an ouster injunction, in practice, advance notice needs to have been given.

Before making an ouster injunction, the judge will want to be satisfied both that the circumstances warrant such an order and that there is no satisfactory alternative in the light of the spouses' conduct and the accommodation available. An ouster injunction will generally be limited to a specific period, such as three months, with a view to enabling a more permanent solution to be reached during this breathing space.

Bear in mind the consequences of seeking and obtaining an ouster injunction in terms of your future relationship: if that is the way your divorce proceedings begin, the prospect of negotiating reasonably and reaching a sensible agreement recedes dramatically.

## registering a right of occupation

The right not to be turned out or kept out of the matrimonial home without a court order against you is binding only on your spouse. You can, however, protect your rights against subsequent buyers or mortgagees by registering your rights: at HM Land Registry if the land is registered, at the Land Charges Department if the land is unregistered.

If you do not register your right and the home is sold, the buyer or mortgagee could turn you out, unless you were living in the home when it was sold or mortgaged and you had not consented to the sale or mortgage taking place.

Rights of occupation (whether registered or not) come to an end on the death of either spouse or when a decree absolute is granted. The court may extend the rights of occupation after the end of the marriage if asked to do so; if you have by then applied for a property adjustment order, this can be registered and will protect you in just the same way.

Although it is possible to register your rights of occupation at any time before the house is actually sold, you should do so as soon as possible because your husband or wife may take steps to sell the home or take out a mortgage on it, without telling you.

Find out, first of all, whether your house has a registered title or not, because there are different ways of registering your rights depending on whether the land is registered or unregistered. An incorrect registration is ineffective.

But it is important that you act quickly. If you are in any doubt or time is short, apply to register at both the Land Registry and the Land Charges Department until you have sorted out the position. If you find that the title is registered you should cancel the charge at the Land Charges Department.

If the house is mortgaged, you can ask the building society or bank to tell you whether the title to your house is registered.

The Land Registry (Lincoln's Inn Fields, London WC2A 3PH telephone 01-405 3488) can be asked whether a particular area is in a district of compulsory registration. Their explanatory leaflet (no. 9) lists the counties and districts in England and

Wales where there is compulsory registration and includes the addresses of the district land registries for the areas.

The land registry for your area will advise you how to make a search to determine whether the particular address is registered, and will also provide details of the necessary forms and procedure for you to register your right.

If the title to the property is not registered, a 'class F' land charge should be registered at the Land Charges Department, Burrington Way, Plymouth PL5 3LP. The form to be used, K2, is available from government bookshops and law stationers shops. The fee for registration is £1.

The information required includes the full name in which the property-owning spouse bought or acquired the property and a description of it. If you are unsure of the precise name shown on the conveyance, register the charge against all possible permutations. The charge is ineffective unless it is in exactly the right name.

The green form scheme allows for a solicitor to deal with registration of a land charge or a notice.

All citizens advice bureaux can help with filling in the forms to register a right of occupation and some have a supply of the necessary forms. It may be quicker to go to a CAB than to get an appointment with a solicitor.

**the effect of registering a charge or notice**
Anyone buying the property or granting a mortgage on it would as a matter of routine check the appropriate registry and discover your notice defending your rights. (Even if a subsequent buyer or mortgagee does not actually search the register or has no knowledge of the registration, the effect of registering a land charge or notice amounts in law to notice of the non-owning spouse's right of occupation.) If he then buys the house or gives the mortgage, he does so subject to your right of occupation and cannot turn you out unless you have agreed to release your rights.

The effect of registration normally ceases once a decree of divorce is made absolute. If the question of the matrimonial home has not been settled by then, the non-owning spouse should ask the court before the decree is made absolute to give permission for the registration of the class F land charge or the notice to be renewed after the decree absolute. A court order for renewal of the registration of a notice or charge must also be protected by registration. Alternatively, if a claim for a property adjustment order has been made (even though it will not have been decided), you should register the existence of the claim.

### moving out

If you hope eventually to have the home to live in permanently, it is tactically best to try to stay there if possible. Even if you are not planning to remain in the long-term but want to persuade your spouse to make other financial provision for you, it may assist you in your negotiations if you stay. However, the strategy of staying put can sometimes be counter-productive: remaining at close quarters with your spouse once the decision to separate has been made, can give rise to tensions which may undermine the prospect of success in negotiating the result you were aiming at. It may be helpful to discuss with your solicitor the pros and cons of moving out, whether on a temporary or permanent basis.

### severing a joint tenancy

If you and your spouse own your home (or any other land or buildings) as joint tenants, the whole property would automatically vest in the survivor should either of you die, irrespective of anything in a will. Either of you can prevent this by sending a 'notice of severance' to the other spouse at any time. This would make you 'tenants in common' and does not affect your status as co-owners, but on death the deceased's share in the property would fall into his or her estate and would be distributed under the terms of his or her will or according to the rules of intestacy.

You may or may not consider that it would be in your interest to sever the joint tenancy; this is something you may like to discuss with a solicitor.

# REACHING A FINANCIAL SETTLEMENT

You and your spouse should discuss and, if possible, agree your financial arrangements, either directly or through solicitors, rather than dissipate your funds and energy by arguments and protracted litigation. Try to understand that the only money available will have to come from what you each have and it has to be shared between you as fairly as possible. If the proceedings become expensive because you argued over every single point, you will have less, and so will your former spouse. Remember that the law cannot create assets which are not there nor spread money farther than it can go.

## a solicitor's help

When going to see a solicitor about the arrangements for the financial terms of your divorce, let the solicitor concentrate on negotiating a settlement and the legal or tax aspects of orders rather than on disentangling the basic information about your practical affairs. Do not expect the solicitor to work out your milk and gas bills or to go rummaging around in three boxes of papers going back ten years.

In order not to waste the solicitor's time and therefore your money, do as much preparation as you can beforehand, so that you can present him or her quickly and concisely with the information that will be needed. Prepare a clear, accurate and complete statement about your financial position and that of your spouse and take with you documents to prove your outgoings.

If you present your lawyer with a list of your assets and liabilities, outgoings and a copy of your proposed budget, you will have saved perhaps one or two hours of the solicitor's time for which you would have been charged.

## information needed for your solicitor or yourself

Whether or not you seek a solicitor's help in trying to agree financial arrangements with your spouse, it is essential that you work out very carefully what your resources are (and those of your spouse) and what your needs are as well as those of your spouse and children – both short-term and long-term.

### 1. details about your home

o who lives there – including adult children, lodgers, dependent relatives
o number of bedrooms, living rooms, bathrooms
o what the rates are (general, sewerage, water)
o who has been paying which household bills
o who has done, or paid for, any work on the house.

You should be prepared to provide figures (as precise as you can) of the necessary expenses of running your home: gas, electricity, telephone, insurance, hire purchase commitments and other regular outgoings.

*if you own your home*

o what is it worth?
  (an approximate estimate)
o when was it bought and for how much?
o how did you arrange your finances to pay for the house?
o who put down the deposit, and what was the source of the
  money?
o what substantial improvements have been made to the
  property since purchase (e.g. central heating)? when? what
  was the cost and how was it paid for?

○ if there is a mortgage:
  – how much is outstanding?
  – what are the monthly payments?
  – when will it be paid off?
  (ask the building society or other lender for any of these facts if you do not know them)
  – if it is an endowment mortgage, when is the policy due to mature and for how much? what is the current surrender/paid-up value of the policy? (ask the insurance company)
  – name, address and account/reference number of the building society, bank or other lender
○ is the house in joint names?
  (this is important – if you find that the house is in your spouse's name only, the house could be sold without your agreement or knowledge but you can take steps to prevent this happening provided that you or your solicitor act quickly)
○ is the title registered?
○ outline information about previous homes:
  – dates of purchase and sale
  – cost price and sale price
  – how the purchases were funded
  – in whose name(s) the properties were bought.

### *if you own a leasehold property*

○ what is the ground rent?
○ what is the service/maintenance charge?
○ how long is the lease?

### *if either you or your spouse own other properties*
(e.g. country cottage, villa abroad, timeshare, all or part of a parent's home) give outline information about its value, and the date and circumstances of its acquisition.

*if you rent your home*

○ is it rented from the council, a housing association, a private landlord?
○ how much rent do you pay? (weekly, monthly, quarterly)
○ is it a regulated tenancy?
○ in whose name is the tenancy? (take along a copy of the tenancy agreement or rent book, if you have one)
○ is there a service or maintenance charge? if so, how much?

## 2. car or other vehicle(s)

○ do you own a car?
 (if so, make, model, year, value)
○ does your spouse own a car?
 (if so, make, model, year, value)
○ will you and/or your spouse need a car in the future?
○ do you or your spouse have the use of a company car?
 if so, what is paid for: tax? insurance? servicing? repairs? petrol?
 what model is it and how often is it replaced?
○ do you and/or your spouse own a
 – motorbike?
 – caravan?
 – boat?
 if so, give make, model, year, value and approximate running costs.

## 3. your own employment

If you are self-employed, you will be required to produce recent accounts, tax returns and tax assessments, generally for the last three years, including draft accounts if the audited accounts are not up to date.

Any regular earnings from occasional freelance or part-time work at home should be listed.

## *if an employee*

o details of your present employment: name of employer, nature of job, whether full or part-time (if currently not employed, details and dates of last employment and qualifications)
o details of additional casual or freelance work
o normal weekly or monthly earnings (produce P.60 form or a copy: this shows gross earnings, tax, national insurance payments and pension contributions for the previous tax year) and at least the last 3 payslips
o any fringe benefits, commission or bonuses regularly received
  e.g. private medical insurance
     subsidised loan
     expense account
     company car
  and a copy of the last 3 years' forms P11D in respect of these benefits.
  These are all relevant: for example, a company car will be treated as 'deeming' you an extra couple of thousand pounds gross income or thereabouts
o expenses of getting to your job and of any clothing and equipment essential for your job
o cost of child-minding or nursery school for child while you are at work
o any other relevant information, such as imminent promotion or redundancy, dates of pay reviews.

Also provide as many of the above details as possible about your spouse's employment and earnings. (Do not worry about the P.60 form – he/she can be asked to produce it in due course.)

## 4. pension

o details of any pension or superannuation scheme to which you belong (occupational or personal plan)

o does pension scheme provide benefit for widow or
  widower? (she/he will probably lose any benefits as a result
  of divorce because of becoming an ex-spouse rather than a
  widow or widower)

Try to obtain a copy of the rules relating to the occupational
pension scheme and an up-to-date statement showing the
present value of your pension.

### 5. other assets and income

o any joint current or savings accounts you have
o your own savings in building society, bank, national savings
  accounts, with details of the account(s) and current bal-
  ance(s)
o stocks and shares and unit trusts, with a current valuation of
  your portfolio (if necessary, ask stockbroker)
o life insurance policy(ies): how much? when maturing?
  (ask the insurance company or broker for current surrender
  values and check whether any policy has been written in
  your spouse's favour)
o the income from your investments over the past two or three
  years e.g. dividends, building society account interest
o valuables, such as jewellery, antiques, with estimates of
  their value and brief details of how they were acquired
  (bought, inherited, gift, etc) and by whom

General house contents are rarely realisable, and proposals
how to divide these between you should be considered separately and generally after outline agreement on the broader
issues has been reached – otherwise, you may get bogged
down in minutiae.

### 6. tax returns

If you have filled in tax returns in the past 3 years, take a copy
of each and copies of all documents referred to in the return,
such as schedules and accounts. Also take copies of any

assessments you have received in the past 3 years for income
tax or capital gains tax (consider whether any of your assets
would result in a capital gains tax liability if disposed of).

## 7. expectancies and trusts

Are you and/or your spouse likely to come into an inheritance
in the foreseeable future? Do either of you have interests under
a trust (perhaps as a result of tax planning by you or your
parents)?

## 8. maintenance

○ maintenance payments (if any) made to your former spouse
  and/or to your child/ren
or
○ children's maintenance payments received from former husband or wife of yourself or your spouse
○ any regular provision to or from someone else e.g. deeds of
  covenant from grandparents

Produce where possible all court orders or maintenance
agreements.

## 9. new partner's finances

If you and/or your spouse are cohabiting with someone else, or
you have plans to marry, you should set out what you know of
that person's financial circumstances.

## 10. payments from DHSS

○ what money do you receive from the DHSS?
  for example:
        supplementary benefit
        family income supplement
        child benefit (including one-parent benefit)
        retirement pension
        invalidity benefit

## 11. debts

Make a list of money you owe: for example, tax arrears, hire purchase, bank overdraft, credit card, other loans.

Note who is responsible for each debt – you or your partner or both of you. You are not responsible for each other's debts. For a loan or credit agreement or other liability which requires payment regularly, note the arrears and the total outstanding.

*joint bank account*
With a joint bank or building society account from which money can be drawn by either of you, there is the risk that the account could be cleared out without the other knowing about it. To prevent this, the bank manager or building society should be told to change the arrangement so that cheques can be drawn only with both signatures.

## expenditure

It is generally difficult to think of where your money goes. Identifying the types of outlay under three headings may help:

o day-to-day spending
o regular payments
o occasional lump sums.

The checklist may include:

babysitter
bank charges
books

cassettes, compact discs
car: insurance, tax, repairs,
   servicing, petrol, oil,
   AA/RAC subscription
childminder
Christmas
cigarettes
clothes

cosmetics (e.g. soap,
   shampoo, chemists' goods)

dentist
drink (at home, pub, club, bar)
dry cleaning

electricity
entertainments (cinema,
   concerts, theatre, bingo)

fares

fees (professional, school, college)
food
fuel (coal, coke, firewood, charcoal)

garden
gas
general household (e.g. lavatory paper, cleaning materials, light bulbs, batteries)
ground rent

hairdresser
help in the home
HP and other credit payments
hobbies
holidays
home decorating and repairs

insurance premiums (car, home, life etc)

launderette/laundry

meals out
medicines, prescriptions
mortgage payments

newspapers, magazines
nursery school fees

oil for central heating
outings for children
overdraft interest

paraffin
payments to dependants

pets (food, vet's bills etc)
photography (films, developing)
pocket money for children
postage stamps
presents
private lessons (e.g. music)
private medical insurance

rates
records and tapes
rent

savings (regular payments)
school meals
season ticket(s)
service charge
servicing and repairs of household equipment (e.g. washing machine, central heating unit)
shoes and shoe repairs
spectacles
sports (equipment, gate money, subscriptions)
stationery and birthday cards
subscriptions to associations, charities, clubs, trade union
sweets, chocolates, icecream

telephone
tools
TV: licence; repairs or rental; video

water charges
window cleaning

Your own checklist should be as complete as possible to be of help to you both. The figures against the items should come from receipted accounts, cheque stubs, credit card statements.

It may be useful to divide your alphabetical list into categories such as home/car/children/etc.

You should also make a note of necessary expenditure that may be looming, such as major car repairs, kitting a child out in new school uniform, and of longer term needs, such as replacing a car, re-roofing the house, and so on.

If you have no idea of how much you do spend on what, get a notebook and write down the cost of your shopping as you unpack it. If your children are old enough to understand, encourage them to note what they spend (it may also make them feel less left out of the future plans which each parent is making).

Not all items will be doubled when you split up: some will be halved, some reduced, some will stay the same and may be paid for by either of you. For instance, electricity will be paid twice, cigarettes and cosmetics divided, school meals and private lessons unchanged. A probable future spending pattern for each of you should emerge from this.

Apart from giving you a better idea of what you both have and what money you are likely to need in the next year or so, this information will be needed for the registrar at the divorce court. By providing this information to a solicitor, you can give him or her a better idea of your financial situation, for the negotiations with your spouse or his or her solicitor.

# viewing the future

By now you are likely to be thoroughly depressed. You will have spent many hours producing meticulous sets of figures and, almost inevitably, they will paint a grim picture. You are likely to wonder how you ever managed to afford living under one roof – let alone how you will juggle two households.

When working out how much money there is and how it should be distributed, remember that your 'resources' list indicates what your income has been recently. But a pay review may be imminent and either of you may have hidden resources – such as an untapped earning capacity, perhaps after retraining.

Go through your current expenditure list, marking on a spare copy how economies might be made in both the short-term and long-term.

Try to consider all the possible alternatives for the future. You strengthen your position by having worked out in detail the actual likely consequences of plans that you and your spouse may each be putting forward, even if (or particularly if) you are convinced that your spouse's suggestions are ridiculously unrealistic.

In practice, you are likely to have little choice and what options there are will be fairly stark. Inevitably you will have to make compromises. It is only by having thought through your priorities that you will be able to mould the eventual compromise into a shape that best suits you and your family.

Making plans for the future revolves primarily around accommodation and income.

**where to live**
Work out what it would cost you to stay on in your home, and where you could move to if you were to move, and how either option would leave you and your spouse financially.

Children's schools, proximity to helpful friends or willing parents – all these can be important considerations, particularly now that you are going to be on your own.

If you own your home, ask one or two local estate agents to tell you what they suggest it might fetch. There should be no charge for this if you explain that you may be selling but have not yet decided. These figures are likely to be on the high side and any purchaser would have a survey done which might reduce the price, but the figures will be a guide. Deduct the likely agents' and conveyancing costs plus the redemption figure for the mortgage and you are left with the 'net equity'. From that, you would have to pay removal costs as well as purchase costs (conveyancing, stamp duty, land registry fees, new carpets, redecoration etc) of possibly two properties – one for each of you. Work out what sort of mortgage you and your spouse could each shoulder and then investigate the property market.

If you are in rented accommodation, and indeed even if you are not, investigate the rented sector – private, council and housing association.

This can be a disheartening business at the best of times but it is only by exploring what might be possibilities that you can work out what are the possibilities, what their respective advantages and disadvantages are and where your priorities lie.

### what to live on

In respect of capital, look at your schedule of resources and work out the net equity in the house (if you own it) and the net value of all other realisable assets after meeting outstanding liabilities (including legal fees). What is realisable will depend upon your circumstances – cashing in a life insurance policy or selling the car might be foolish in some circumstances but unavoidable in others. Everyday household belongings are rarely realisable and should preferably be linked to need – the parent with the children, for example, is likely to need the washing machine, and indeed the majority of the furnishings. The other parent, however, may need to buy, either immediately or in due course, his or her own household equipment and furniture.

Similarly, in respect of income, work out what you would each be left with if, for example, the wife were to receive maintenance to 'top up' her own earnings to one third of the couple's joint gross incomes and the husband were to pay each of the children a certain level of periodical payments (to be spent by their mother on looking after them).

*calculation for one-third starting point*

| Husband | £ | £ |
|---|---|---|
| gross monthly pay | | . . . . . |

*less:*

| | | |
|---|---|---|
| national insurance | . . . . . | |
| pension contribution (if compulsory) | . . . . . | |
| travel to work | . . . . . | . . . . . |
| | | (A) |

| Wife | | |
|---|---|---|
| gross monthly pay | | . . . . . |
| child benefit | | . . . . . |

*less:*

| | | |
|---|---|---|
| national insurance | . . . . . | |
| pension contributions (if compulsory) | . . . . . | |
| childminder | . . . . . | |
| travel to work | . . . . . | . . . . . |
| | | (B) |

| | |
|---|---|
| total combined income (A + B) divided by 3 | . . . . . |
| less (B) | . . . . . |

starting point for order would be: $\dfrac{A + B}{3} - B = £$ . . . . .

The one-third starting point is simply that: a starting point. It is most certainly not a golden rule and how to calculate the one-third starting point is itself not a cast iron formula.

If school bills are being met by one spouse, the gross cost of these is usually deducted along with national insurance and compulsory pension contributions. If one spouse has fringe benefits such as a company car or a lot of business entertaining, he or she will be 'deemed' extra gross income – for a company car, perhaps £1,500 or so upwards per annum.

After having considered the one-third starting point, look at it from a 'net effect' point of view, combined with estimates of each spouse's realistic needs.

*'net effect' calculations*

| Husband | £ | Wife | £ |
|---|---|---|---|
| gross income: | | gross income: | |
| earnings | | earnings | |
| any other income | | any other income | |
| | | child benefit | |
| | | payments from husband | |
| | | children's periodical | |
| | | payments | |
| *less:* | | *less:* | |
| tax | | tax | |
| national insurance | | national insurance | |
| contributions | | contributions | |
| pension | | pension contributions | |
| contributions | | travel to work | |
| periodical payments | | | |
| to wife | | | |
| periodical payments | | | |
| to children | | | |
| travel to work | | | |
| Available income | £ | Available income | £ |

These figures compared with your forecast of your needs may show that one or both of you has got nowhere near enough to meet your projected expenses. Looking at your incomes, needs and available capital (if any), a decision must be reached on how things can be arranged to come up with more realistic figures. In many cases, it will just have to be accepted that both of you are going to be very hard up, at least for a while.

**negotiating a settlement**
Your objective must be to negotiate a workable financial settlement with your spouse.

Depending on your circumstances, you may choose to see a solicitor for a preliminary discussion after which you and your spouse might be able to reach a provisional agreement. Each of you may then think it wise to return to your respective solicitors to discuss your proposed arrangements, with a view to having these embodied in a formal separation agreement or court order. Alternatively, you may feel that it would be best for negotiations to be conducted between the solicitors. In either case, you will need to be aware of how the court would be likely to reach a decision if it came to a hearing.

*separation agreement*
If you and your spouse want to separate but have no plans to divorce, it is not essential to institute formal judicial separation proceedings . Couples can make a separation agreement or get a deed of separation drawn up by a solicitor in which they record formally what financial arrangements have been reached. Such arrangements are legally enforceable and can be as tax-efficient in providing for a spouse (but not for children) as a court order.

It would be wise for each partner to obtain independent legal advice before entering into a binding agreement. Courts take separation agreements extremely seriously, and an agreement that is intended to be binding, which was reached after full financial disclosure and especially if each party had a solicitor's advice, will be upheld by a court unless very good reason is shown why that would be quite unjust. Variation of an agreed maintenance provision is, however, possible if circumstances change significantly and, if your spouse will not agree, you can ask the court to order a variation.

# orders the divorce court can make

Any of the orders the court can make for financial provision on divorce may be made by consent between the parties or can be imposed after a contested hearing.

## for periodical payments

An order for periodical payments can be made any time after the decree nisi, but does not come into force until the decree absolute. (An order for maintenance pending suit can cover the period from petition to decree absolute.) The order may be expressed as £xx per week/month/year, as the case may be, to be paid to the ex-spouse and/or the children.

If the order does not say whether the money is due in advance or in arrears, it is payable monthly in arrears, with the first payment being due one month after the date the order says it is 'with effect from'.

Orders may be backdated to the date of the application which led to the order in question (whether or not by consent) and arrears may then immediately be due. (Credit is given for payments made 'on account' between the date of the application and the order.) Such backdating can be effective for tax purposes and is one reason why it can be sensible to file an application at an early stage in negotiations, even if you expect to reach an out-of-court settlement.

An order for periodical payments to a spouse ceases automatically on the recipient's marriage or on the death of either the payer or the recipient.

The order may specify a limited period only – say, 2 years – if, for example, all that is needed is maintenance for a brief period to enable one spouse, generally the wife, to find her feet. The court can direct that no further application for periodical payments may then be made.

The court can be asked to vary (that is, change the amount of) an order for periodical payments if a change in circumstances warrants it. But if an application for periodical payments has been dismissed, it cannot be revived.

Orders for children are generally made to run until each child reaches the age of 17 or ceases full-time education, whichever is the later, or until a further order is made. It may be worth considering limiting the duration to school education only, because a court order might prejudice grant entitlement for further education – effectively reducing a grant £ for £ in respect of the child's income beyond a certain minimum threshold.

*secured payments*
The court has power to order that periodical payments be 'secured' by a capital asset that the paying party possesses. A secured order is rare and is only relevant where there is a lot of available capital. It should not be contemplated without legal advice. A secured order can last for the life of the recipient because it survives the death of the payer; no other maintenance order does so.

**for adjustment of property**
The divorce court has wide powers to deal with the couple's property. 'Property' is used for any asset, such as a car or items of furniture, not just an owner-occupied matrimonial home and not just assets acquired in the course of the marriage.

A variety of orders can be made re-distributing the assets and the matrimonial home.

The court can, for example

○ order the transfer of possessions from single or joint owner-ship to one or other of the spouses
○ order the home to be sold and the proceeds of sale to be divided in such proportions as the court thinks appropriate
○ give one party the right to stay on in the matrimonial home until a certain date or event, the house then to be sold and the proceeds divided
○ transfer ownership of the home outright from one spouse to the other
○ transfer a tenancy from one spouse to the other.

**for a lump sum**
This is precisely what it says: an order that one person pays an amount of cash to the other, now or at some time in the future. A lump sum is a once-and-for-all payment which cannot be varied nor asked for a second time.

A lump sum order may be made if one of the couple has large assets that are readily realisable in cash, such as stocks and shares, or if one spouse can raise money on the security of other assets, such as a business.

If there is presently no scope for a lump sum order but there is a real possibility of capital arising in the foreseeable future, the application for a lump sum can be adjourned with 'liberty to apply' later.

The court sometimes makes a lump sum order when one spouse is to buy out the other's interest in the former matrimonial home. A wealthy wife may be ordered to pay a lump sum to her husband, perhaps to enable him to buy a house, just as a wealthy husband can be ordered to pay a lump sum to his wife.

The court can order the lump sum payment to be made by instalments and, if necessary, application can subsequently be made to vary how the instalments are paid (but not to change the overall total). The court can also order that interest be paid in case of deferment or default.

A court does not have power to make an order for a lump sum or property adjustment in favour of a former spouse who has remarried unless he or she made the application for such an order before the new marriage.

A lump sum can be awarded to either party in addition to or instead of maintenance payments.

*instead of maintenance*
Where the husband has substantial capital available, a lump sum payment to the wife can take the place of maintenance for her, wholly or partially (as can a property adjustment order transferring the home to the wife). A lump sum payment helps to remove the bitterness which periodical payments can cause: once the capital payment is made, the parties can regard the

book as closed. Such a final order, with no continuing maintenance obligations to a former spouse, is known as a 'clean break'.

From the husband's point of view, one lump sum payment instead of making periodical payments to his former wife may well be attractive. However, if she marries again only a short while after receiving a substantial lump sum in lieu of maintenance, the ex-husband would have no redress. But if the wife at the time of the order knew of her impending marriage and did not disclose it, the husband might be able to appeal.

A lump sum payment in lieu of periodical payments is not always ideal for the recipient. Periodical payments tend to bear a fairly direct relationship to the payer's earnings and the order can be taken to the court from time to time for review as and when circumstances change – whereas a lump sum order cannot be added to.

### for children
Lump sum payments to children can also be ordered but, in practice, they are rarely made.

### side-effects of a lump sum
If the recipient of a lump sum is legally aided, a lump sum of over £2,500 may be reduced by the legal aid fund's statutory charge.

And if the lump sum brings the recipient's total capital above the limit for getting legal aid, the legal aid certificate may be withdrawn even if there are other legal matters still needing a solicitor, so that the further work remaining to be done by the solicitor will have to be paid by the client personally.

Similarly, a lump sum payment may put the recipient outside the supplementary benefit limits.

### deliberately disposing of assets
If the wife fears or suspects that the husband, in order to avoid making proper financial provision for her or the children, is getting rid of assets (possibly to a woman with whom he is

living, or into a bank account abroad) or is deliberately wasting capital by living extravagantly, she should immediately apply to the divorce court for an order preventing her husband from disposing of assets or for an order setting aside any disposal which has taken place. In support of her application, she would have to provide an affidavit giving all the relevant facts. (Husbands also can, and do, make such an application.)

The court will assume that the proposed or actual disposition was carried out with the intention of preventing the wife or children obtaining payment where such a disposition has taken place within the three years prior to the application, or is about to take place, and has had or would have the effect of defeating the claim for financial relief – unless the husband can prove the contrary.

A disposition – for instance, the sale of a house – will not be set aside, however, if the buyer acted in good faith, paid the full value and was unaware of the seller's intentions. But if the property was sold for less than the true value, the judge may consider this an indication of collusion between husband and buyer, and may be able to set the sale aside. Alternatively, it may be possible to obtain an order 'freezing' the sale proceeds.

## giving information to each other

Before either you or your spouse can put forward serious proposals for financial arrangements, you must have a clear picture of your financial position and that of your spouse. You each have a duty to give full and frank disclosure of all material facts. These can include not just your current income and capital but any plans you may have to marry or set up home with someone else, an anticipated legacy from a recently deceased relative or the prospect of significantly better results from your business when the latest accounts are produced.

Just how serious is the obligation was shown by the recent House of Lords decision in the case of Jenkins v Livesey. In that case, decree absolute was pronounced in April, terms of agreement were reached in August and about one week later the wife became engaged to be married without telling the court or her ex-husband. On 2 September, an order was made by consent; on 22 September in accordance with the order, the husband transferred his half share in the home to the wife, who, two days later married. In these circumstances, the court order was held to be invalid for lack of proper disclosure and the ex-husband was entitled to have it set aside.

These circumstances were somewhat exceptional. You would not be able to have an order set aside on the grounds of failure to disclose some minor matter which would not have made any difference to the order that the court would have made.

### proposals

When you are satisfied that you have a clear view of the overall financial picture, you can put forward proposals for settlement, on a 'without prejudice' basis. This means that if the proposals do not result in settlement and litigation does ensue, they cannot be referred to in making submissions to the judge or registrar. Usually it is the spouse who will be paying maintenance and/or a lump sum who puts forward the first proposals; frequently (but not always) these result in counter proposals from the other spouse. Generally, the eventual agreement will fall somewhere between these two sets of proposals.

You may therefore be tempted to pitch your first proposals very low (or very high as the case may be). This is on the whole not a good idea. Although whatever proposals you make may be interpreted as just an opening bid, unrealistic proposals will sour the atmosphere and prolong the agony, with inevitable consequences in terms of both acrimony and legal costs. They are also likely to prompt your spouse into being equally unrealistic when it comes to counter proposals and you will be faced with what appears to be an unbridgeable gulf.

#### compromising
Carefully timed, carefully considered and realistic proposals should mean that there is not too wide a gap between you. The question then is, how to close the gap altogether. Look at the net effect calculations, consider tax effectiveness and put yourself in your partner's shoes. You have the advantage of knowing your spouse well and you are likely to know what will be attractive and what will be abhorrent.

Ultimately, you may simply have to split the difference between you and/or reach a bargain over household goods to offset an imbalance in terms of hard cash. Reaching a compromise, however, should not mean bullying your spouse into submission or allowing yourself to be bullied. If you feel this is happening, talk about it with your solicitor. Similarly, if you feel that your spouse is not giving full disclosure or is deliberately disposing of assets, make your worries clear to your solicitor without delay – the court does have powers to deal with tactics such as these.

#### barristers' adjudication
If you really cannot reach agreement, you may like to discuss with your solicitor the possibility of putting all the papers before a barrister who would act as an arbitrator and would tell both you and your spouse what he or she thinks would be a reasonable framework for settlement.

The solicitors for both of you can together arrange to obtain a confidential 'Recommendation' from a barrister acting as an adjudicator of the Family Law Bar Association Conciliation Board. It is a kind of informal arbitration, but the parties are not bound to accept the recommendation unless they have expressly agreed to do so either before or after receiving it. The procedure can only be made use of if both parties agree and if they are each represented by a solicitor (barristers cannot take instructions directly from the public). The intervention of a neutral and experienced outsider might nudge you towards a settlement and might avoid or limit costly and often unsatisfactory negotiations.

The FLBA Conciliation Board fees for a recommendation are

on a standard scale. In cases not involving substantial capital other than the matrimonial home, the fee is £85. Where substantial capital, trusts or business accounts are involved, it is likely to be £150. The fee for particularly complex cases will be a matter for negotiation. A legal aid certificate does not cover obtaining a recommendation under the scheme so even if you are legally aided, you will yourself have to pay your solicitor's charges for arranging to obtain a recommendation, as well as the FLBA fee.

The rules and application forms for a recommendation can be obtained by your solicitor from the FLBA Conciliation Board at 4 Paper Buildings, Temple, London EC4Y 7EX.

The scheme is a recent one and how effective it will be in practice is not yet known.

# reaching an agreement

When you do reach an agreement, you may decide not to record it at all, or you may decide to set it out in the form of a written document, or you may decide to have it embodied in a court order.

On the whole, if you are getting divorced, it is in your interests to ask the court to make an order by consent in the terms that you have agreed. A court order is easier to enforce and is the only route to tax efficiency for maintenance payments to children. If the recipient wants to obtain a mortgage, this may be difficult to arrange unless maintenance is being paid under a court order.

Also, it is only through a court order that financial claims can be dealt with on a final basis.

It is advisable for each of you to have a solicitor's help in going through the proposed arrangements and drafting a deed or agreement or order recording them. One solicitor cannot act for both of you and either may advise that the terms do not seem satisfactory. Your solicitor has a duty to give you this kind of advice and although you do not have to act on it, you should consider it carefully.

## applying for a consent order

An application can be made at any time by a couple for an order to be made by consent for maintenance pending suit and interim periodical payments for children. For a final order, the application cannot be made before you apply for 'directions for trial' under the special procedure, and the order will not be made until the decree nisi has been pronounced.

Make sure that you are content with the agreed terms before applying to the court for a final order. A solicitor should be able to ensure that the form of the order is as comprehensive, watertight, and tax-efficient as possible. And, before lodging the application, make sure that you have given full disclosure of your circumstances and that, so far as you can tell, your spouse has done so, too. A consent order can be applied for without filing affidavits but you will each have to supply a short synopsis of your circumstances, known as a 'Rule 76(A) Statement' (a form is obtainable from the divorce court office).

Rule 76(A) of the Matrimonial Causes Rules provides that a statement of information shall include

(a) the duration of the marriage, the age of each party and of any minor or dependent child of the family;

(b) an estimate in summary form of the approximate amount or value of the capital resources and net income of each party and of any minor child of the family;

(c) what arrangements are intended for the accommodation of each of the parties and any minor child of the family;

(d) whether either party has remarried or has any present intention to marry or to cohabit with another person;

(e) where the terms of the order provide for the transfer of property a statement confirming that any mortgagee of that property has been served with notice of the application and that no objection to such a transfer has been made by the mortgagee within 14 days from such service; and

(f) any other especially significant matters.

The statement could be along the lines of the following form issued by the Divorce Registry.

**FAMILY DIVISION**

**PRINCIPAL REGISTRY**

Between _____ Petitioner

and _____ Respondent

| | Statement of information for a consent order |

**Date of marriage:**

**Ages of**

Petitioner _____ Respondent _____
Minor (i.e under the age of 18) or dependent children

_____  _____  _____  _____  _____  _____

**Note**

If the application is only for an order for interim periodical payments or variation of an order for periodical payments then only the information required under "net income" need be given.

**Summary of means**

Give approximate amount or value of capital resources and net income of petitioner and respondent and, where relevant, of minor children of the family.

| | Capital resources (less any unpaid mortgage or charge) | Net income |
|---|---|---|
| Petitioner | | |
| Respondent | | |
| Children | | |

D667

**Where the parties are to live**
Give details of what arrangements are intended for the
accommodation of each of the parties and any minor child(ren)
of the family.

**Marital plans**
If either party has remarried or has any **present** intention to
marry or to cohabit with another person tick the correct box
below

Petitioner        Respondent

☐                 ☐                 has remarried

☐                 ☐                 intends to remarry

☐                 ☐                 intends to cohabit with another person

To be answered
by the **applicant**
where the terms
of the order
provide for a
transfer of prop-
erty.

**Notice to mortgagee**
Has ny and every mortgagee of the property been served with
notice of the application?

                    Yes ☐    No ☐

Has any objection to such a transfer been made by any mortgagee
within 14 days from the date of service?

                    Yes ☐    No ☐

**Other information**
Give details of any other especially significant matters.

**Signatures**

Signed _____        Signed _____
(solicitor for) Petitioner    (Solicitor for) Respondent

Date _____               Date _____

Address all communications to the Chief Clerk and quote the above case number
The court office at

is open from 10am to 4pm Monday to Friday only.

Provided the registrar has sufficient information to be satisfied that the proposed terms are reasonable and both parties are in agreement, he is likely to accept the agreement and issue a formal consent order as requested. If the agreement is put forward by solicitors on each side, the registrar may approve it without either of you having to attend in person but, if you are acting for yourself, the registrar will probably make an appointment to discuss the proposed order with you and your spouse, and may require further evidence, especially if no affidavits have been filed.

**form of consent order**
An order made by consent can be much more comprehensive than an order made after a contested hearing. This is because you and your spouse can include undertakings (formal promises) in respect of matters over which the court could make no order: for example, an undertaking by a husband to make payments by standing order, to supply completed certificates of deduction of income tax quarterly, to arrange the transfer to his wife of a car owned by a company of which he has control – and so on. Undertakings are enforceable, so make sure that you do not undertake to do anything which might turn out to be impossible.

You can also include 'recitals' setting out the background to the order: for example, that you intend it to be in full and final settlement of any claims, including those under the Married Women's Property Act 1882 and the Inheritance (Provision for Family and Dependants) Act 1975, or, for example, noting 'for the record' that the matrimonial home has been sold and the proceeds divided (and, by implication, taken into account in the overall settlement).

And do not forget to include reference to costs, whether for payment by one party of the other's costs or 'no order for costs', and deal, too, with orders for costs 'reserved' on interim applications.

The words 'liberty to apply' are sometimes written into the wording of consent orders. The effect of this is to allow either of the couple to go back to the court for implementation of the order. It does not allow either party to seek in any way to vary the terms of an order for a lump sum or a property adjustment order.

Another common provision is that where an order is intended to be final, the order states that each agrees that all other claims made by either of them are formally dismissed. Before a claim can be dismissed, it has to have been made and therefore the application for a consent order is generally accompanied by an application raising all financial claims of husband and wife that have not already been raised; they are made only so that they can be dismissed.

But do not agree to a consent order thinking that you might be able to have it set aside subsequently – it is rarely the case that circumstances warrant this. You can apply to have a consent order set aside only on grounds of

o fresh evidence that could not have been known at the time
o fundamental mistakes such as wholly erroneous information on which all parties, including the court, relied
o fraud (which may include evidence that the other party had no intention of ever abiding by the terms of the order)
o lack of full and frank disclosure if such disclosure would have resulted in an order substantially different to that which was made.

# PROCEDURE FOR OBTAINING FINANCIAL ORDERS

An application by the petitioner for financial provision should be made in the petition; the respondent can make an application in the answer if defending or by issuing a notice of application if he or she does not file an answer. Leave of the court must be obtained before an application can be made by the petitioner for a request that was not in the petition, and also by a respondent who is defending if the request was not made in the answer. Applications can only be made in any event if the applicant has not married again.

### after divorce in another country
A court in England or Wales can make orders for financial provision in cases where a marriage has been dissolved or annulled or the parties to the marriage have been legally separated by judicial or other proper proceedings outside the British Isles.

Leave to pursue such an application has first to be obtained from the High Court which has to decide according to the domicile and other circumstances of the applicant whether this country would be an appropriate jurisdiction to hear the application. An affidavit setting out all the circumstances must be filed with the request for leave to apply. It would be advisable to consult a solicitor before embarking on this.

### after separation
Where a divorce is sought after a separation of five years or more, or on the basis of consent after a separation of at least two years, the respondent can indicate in the acknowledgment

of service that he or she intends to apply to the court to consider what his or her financial position will be after the divorce.

A special form of application for the court to consider the respondent's financial position after the divorce can be obtained from the court office. It must be filed at the court to enable the respondent to gain the protection of these proceedings (the indication in the acknowledgment of service is not sufficient).

The decree cannot then be made absolute unless the registrar is satisfied that the petitioner is going to make fair and reasonable financial provision for the respondent, or the best that can be made in the circumstances.

## the orders

An application can be made for all or any of the following:

o  an order for maintenance pending suit
o  a periodical payments order
o  a lump sum order
o  an order for secured provision
o  a property adjustment order.

The question of money is generally dealt with separately from that of the divorce in that the divorce proceedings are usually resolved before finances are. When financial matters drag on, especially if they end up in a hearing, it may be many months or even years before they are finally sorted out. As time is money and you are likely to be instructing solicitors, this is bound to be expensive.

A legal aid certificate covers work in connection with financial applications, including representation at the hearing.

*when there has been maintenance pending suit*
An order for maintenance pending suit will cease when the decree is made absolute. Before this happens, the person receiving the maintenance should write to the court to ask for

the order to be changed into a periodical payments order at the same rate (unless he or she wants to apply for an order for a different amount). The court gives notice of this to the payer. If he does not object, an order for periodical payments at the same rate is made without a hearing before the registrar.

If the payer does object, an appointment will be made for both sides to attend a hearing at which the registrar will decide the amount of the periodical payments to be ordered. Affidavits should be filed before the hearing, with up-to-date information about means.

# making an application

Although an application other than for maintenance pending suit and interim periodical payments for children will not be considered by the court until the decree nisi stage, you should consider filing your application for financial provision as early in the proceedings as possible. This can enable payments to be backdated to the date of the application and retrospective tax relief may be obtained. Make it plain to your spouse, either directly or through solicitors, that this should not be interpreted as an unwillingness to try to negotiate an agreement. On the contrary, by setting out your own financial position in an affidavit supporting the application, you are paving the way to productive negotiations.

If you are the petitioner (or a respondent who is defending), you apply by *Notice of intention to proceed with application for ancillary relief made in petition*; if you are the respondent, by *Notice of application for ancillary relief*. Both forms are available free from divorce court offices.

Two copies of the notice of application have to be completed (and keep an extra one for yourself) and both have to be lodged at the court office. They must be accompanied by an affidavit in support of your application. The fee for lodging an application for ancillary relief is at present £15.

There is space on the application form for the date of the hearing: this will be filled in by the court office.

List the orders you are seeking. Do not state the amounts for the maintenance payments or lump sum claimed: these will be decided during negotiations or at the hearing.

Where the application includes a property adjustment claim, the address of the house or flat or description of any other property which you wish to be transferred should be given with particulars, so far as you know, of any mortgage, whether the title to the property is registered or unregistered and the title number if it is registered. If there is a mortgage, the mortgagees (building society or bank) will have to be sent a copy of the application and, if they request it, a copy of the affidavit in support of the application.

Standard forms of affidavit may be obtained from the divorce court office or, for a few pence, from law stationers shops. (You do not have to use the standard form but it is a useful guide to the relevant information to be given in your own affidavit.) The affidavit should be completed in triplicate, the top copy lodged at the court, one copy sent to the other spouse, and one for you to keep. If there is already in existence a magistrates' court order for the maintenance of the other spouse or children, a copy should be sent with the affidavit to the divorce court.

The application will be sealed at the court office and handed back to you. You must then send a copy of the application to your spouse (together with a copy of the affidavit you lodged with the application), within four days. Use recorded delivery or get a certificate of posting from the counter clerk at the post office. If your spouse does not turn up at the hearing, you will have to satisfy the court that the copy application was sent.

The notice of application requires the other spouse to file an affidavit of his or her means within 14 days of receiving the notice of application.

Once an application for a property adjustment order has been made, you can register a 'pending action' against the title to the property, which may be useful if the registration of your right to occupy the matrimonial home is about to be overtaken by decree absolute or if the property in question is not jointly owned by you and is not the matrimonial home.

## the affidavits

The basis of the evidence set before the registrar is contained in the affidavits sworn by each spouse. It is therefore important to make sure that the information in your own affidavit is complete and accurate and gives all the information that the registrar is likely to require. It is equally important to ensure that your spouse discloses all relevant information.

Affidavits are written in the first person and in concise numbered paragraphs. It is not necessary to go into very detailed explanation and you should avoid hearsay information which was not given to you directly. You should include the paragraph 'Save as set out above, I have no other source of capital or income.' – and it should be true.

Remember that an affidavit is made on oath and false statements amount to perjury.

Clear and accurate details should be given of your own capital and income and liabilities as well as what you know of the financial position of anyone you may be planning to marry or live with. It will be helpful for the court if at this stage you set out your needs in the form of a budget, putting outgoings on a common weekly or monthly basis and giving a total – but you may consider that, from the point of view of ongoing negotiations with your spouse, tactically this would be best left until later.

As much information as possible should be given about any property you want to have transferred to you: its value, when it was bought, and the price paid for it.

For a house, whether or not you want to have it transferred to you, details should be given of any mortgages on it (including any insurance policy which is collateral security for a mortgage) and the amount still owing to the mortgagees.

Where several houses have been owned during the marriage, try to give details of each and the dates of purchase and sale (approximately), the prices paid and obtained for each property and the contributions made by each spouse to the purchase (including loans or gifts by in-laws) or to the improvement of each home.

Also include any information you have about your spouse's other property.

*property valuations*
You may include in your affidavit an estimate of the value of any property you or your spouse own.

You may have asked a local estate agent to tell you what a reasonable asking price would be for your home, but your spouse may think that the value is over (or under) optimistic. It is then generally best, if possible, to agree to instruct one valuer to carry out a formal valuation – for which you will have to pay a fee – agreeing that you will each accept what that valuer says. Otherwise, if you each instruct a separate valuer, their reports may disagree; if there is then a contested hearing, each may have to be called as a witness (adding to the costs) and the court will have to decide what value to attribute.

If there is delay before the application comes to court, it may be necessary to get the valuation updated.

**information in your affidavit**
It is usually helpful to attach to the affidavit copies of several recent payslips and of your P60 (the form issued to all employees at the end of each tax year, giving details of gross pay and tax deducted). If you are self-employed, at least your three most recent sets of accounts should be attached.

If yours is the first affidavit, you can set out what you know of your spouse's finances, especially areas which you think might be forgotten, such as valuable personal belongings or fringe benefits. If yours is the second to be filed, you can comment on any omissions or inaccuracies in the other's affidavit.

**information from your spouse**

When you receive a copy of your spouse's affidavit, go through it carefully to see whether he or she has omitted any major assets or sources of income.

You can reply to specific inaccuracies or points made, by filing a third affidavit. If allegations were made which you believe to be false, these should also be commented on in a further affidavit – but do not let the number of affidavits spiral uncontrollably. (The court may give directions limiting the number that can be filed without the court's explicit consent.)

If your spouse 'puts you to proof' of information, you must provide this and may do so in an affidavit.

If you want to check, investigate or clarify information given to you in an affidavit, write and ask for this information. Rule 77(4) of the Matrimonial Causes Rules 1977 states: 'Any party to an application for ancillary relief may by letter require any other party to give further information concerning any matter contained in any affidavit filed by or on behalf of that other party or any other relevant matter, or to furnish a list of relevant documents or to allow inspection of any such document . . .'

It is quite usual to ask for this kind of supplementary information and documentation. What it is appropriate to ask for depends very much on how comprehensive the other person's affidavit is and how complicated the finances are. Requests may be made, for example, for

o copy pay slips for, say, the past 3 months
o copy form P.60
o copy forms P11D, tax returns and notices of assessment for the past 3 years
o copy contract of employment or statement of terms of employment

o copy bank statements and building society passbooks for, say, the past 12 months
o statements of current surrender values of insurance policies
o statement of value of pension scheme and copy of pension rules
o valuations of antiques, jewellery etc (market value not insurance value).

If the information or documentation is not supplied, you can then apply to the registrar asking him to order your spouse to provide such information or documents. Whether or not you will be successful in obtaining such an order depends on the reasonableness of the request in the circumstances.

Just as it is usual to make an application to the court for financial relief even though you hope to negotiate an out-of-court settlement, it is also quite usual to make requests in the form of a 'questionnaire' (a list of questions stated to be a formal request under Rule 77(4)) in order to clarify the financial picture before proposals are made or agreed. If no agreement is ultimately reached, a spare copy of the questionnaire and answers should be made available for the court.

If your spouse has failed to file an affidavit and you think he or she is going to continue to be difficult about this, do not allow matters to drift on too long; delaying may be a deliberate tactic. You can apply to the registrar for an order requiring that an affidavit be filed within a set period and to have what is known as a 'penal notice' endorsed on the order. If this is done and a copy of the order is served personally on your spouse, he or she will be in contempt of court if still failing to comply, and an application can be made to the judge to commit him or her to prison.

*interim order*

If your affidavit contains some reasonably up-to-date information about your spouse's financial position, this may enable the registrar to make at least an interim order even if your spouse has failed to file an affidavit in time.

If the wife has some evidence as to the husband's income and he does not file his affidavit or does not attend a hearing, the registrar could make an interim order based on her estimate of the husband's income and a general assessment of his likely liabilities.

If the husband is clearly not cooperating at all, the registrar might well make a high interim order for periodical payments with the deliberate aim of forcing him to disclose his means in order to obtain a reduction of the order.

An interim order can be replaced by a lower (or higher) order backdated to take effect from the date of the interim order.

## 'directions' and preliminary hearing

Notification of the date of the hearing is sent by the court to both parties. It is important to be clear as to the nature of the hearing – preliminary or full. If unsure, make a telephone call to the clerk's office at the court to ask.

There will generally first be an appointment for 'directions', at which the registrar gives directions about further steps that need to be taken. This preliminary hearing may be coupled with a hearing for maintenance pending suit, if the court has adequate information to make such an order.

Some courts now issue standard directions (for example, as to when affidavits must be filed, how an owner-occupied home should be valued) automatically on the filing of a financial application.

You yourself can apply for a hearing for directions if one has not been fixed – for instance, if your spouse has failed to comply with any request you had made under Rule 77(4), or had failed to file an affidavit. Or you may want an interim order for maintenance. (If the registrar feels that such a hearing was unnecessary, he may order you to pay your spouse's costs or expenses in attending the hearing.)

At a directions hearing, the registrar will not make a decision about the application (unless it is for an agreed or interim order) but will be concerned to ensure that the necessary steps have been or will be taken so that all the required information will be available to the court at the eventual hearing.

The registrar can make orders for further affidavits or that there shall be no further affidavits without leave, for information or documents to be supplied, for discovery of documents relevant to the applications, for either or both parties to give oral evidence, for valuation. Cohabitants cannot be ordered to file affidavits but either party may issue a witness summons requiring him or her to attend for examination at the final hearing if this seems necessary for the court to have a full financial picture. The cohabitant may apply to be given leave to file an affidavit instead.

If you want to be sure that your spouse will be present at the full hearing to give evidence, ask at the preliminary hearing for the registrar to make an order that he or she should attend for cross-examination.

# the hearing

Before a contested hearing, you should prepare for your own use (and/or for your solicitor) a summary of the financial position of each of you. From your joint gross income, work out the one-third starting figure, noting down any factors which you feel should in your case increase or decrease this starting point. Also work out the net effect of any order you plan to propose and have a budget available setting out your own reasonable needs. Such information will help you to present your case clearly to the registrar; it will be useful to take along a copy to hand to him.

People who are dealing with their own case have to attend the hearing before the registrar. Make sure to take all the relevant documents with you including copies of all affidavits and any questionnaires. Even if you are represented by a lawyer, you are usually expected to be present to give evidence if required and to hear the registrar's decision.

The hearing is 'in chambers' – that is, not open to the public. Each spouse has an opportunity to state his or her case, either in person and/or through a solicitor.

You may have to give oral evidence on oath, if only to bring your affidavit up-to-date. When there is oral evidence, the applicant gives evidence first and can be cross-examined by the other party – who can similarly be cross-examined on his or her evidence, if appropriate.

When oral evidence is not asked for, both sides can make submissions or comments after the affidavits are read, but neither is subject to cross-examination.

## how the court decides

Before deciding on the amount of **maintenance** to order, the registrar will take into account

- the gross income of the husband
- any necessary expenses of his work that can properly be set against his gross income
- the gross income of the wife
- any necessary expenses of her work that can properly be set against her gross income
- the needs of the children, now and in the foreseeable future
- broad details of the expense of maintaining the children
- the needs and outgoings of husband and of wife
- the net effect of, and any particular circumstances that might lead to departure from, the one-third starting point
- the possibility of each being financially self-sufficient (a 'clean break')
- the effect of tax on any proposed order
- the effect of any order on supplementary benefit entitlement.

When dealing with a request for a **property adjustment** or a **lump sum** order (which may or may not be at the same hearing as for maintenance), the registrar will consider

- the full extent of each party's capital and details of any other assets
- the value of the matrimonial home, and any other properties owned by either the husband or the wife or by both
- the amount owing on any mortgages
- the needs of each for accommodation
- who has care and control of the children
- the financial contributions or other contributions made by each towards the purchase or improvement of the matrimonial home and any previous homes
- if husband or wife is legally aided, the effect of the legal aid fund's statutory charge on a property adjustment or lump sum order.

In deciding whether to make financial orders on a divorce and if so what orders, the court must have regard to all the circumstances of the case, giving first consideration to the welfare of any child of the family who is under 18.

Statutory guidelines require the court to take account of:

o the income, earning capacity, property and other financial resources of you and your spouse both now and in the foreseeable future, including any increased earning capacity which the court could reasonably expect either of you to try and acquire
o the financial needs, obligations and responsibilities of you and your spouse both now and in the foreseeable future
o your standard of living before the breakdown of the marriage
o your ages
o the length of the marriage
o any physical or mental disabilities
o the contributions of each of you to the welfare of the family including any contribution in caring for the family or looking after the home, both in the past and in the foreseeable future
o in some circumstances, your or your spouse's conduct
o the value of any benefit, such as a pension, which either of you would lose the chance of acquiring as a result of the divorce.

These guidelines are set out in Section 25 of the Matrimonial Causes Act 1973, as amended by the Matrimonial and Family Proceedings Act 1984. The 1984 Act altered the previous guidelines in various ways and specifically directed that the court must give first consideration to the welfare of any child of the family under 18 when considering all the circumstances of a case. In practice, the needs of dependent children had long determined what course the court could reasonably follow in making appropriate orders, but the specific endorsement of this principle gives recognition to the role of the parent with whom the children make their main base while also discouraging any assumption that that parent is automatically entitled to life-long support without further question, purely as a result of having looked after the children.

The old objective that the court should try to place the parties in the financial position they would have been in if the marriage had not broken down, so far as it was practicable and just to do so, has been abolished. In any case, it was rare that a couple's finances could ever stretch far enough to reach this goal. The thrust of the guidelines is now more clearly forward-looking – but only after taking careful note of all the circumstances relating to the marriage and the family. The court must still consider the standard of living enjoyed before the breakdown when considering appropriate provision for the future.

### earning capacity

The court is now specifically directed to consider whether either spouse could reasonably increase his or her earning capacity. The 1984 Act reflects what was already a definite thread both in contested cases and in out-of-court settlements – the desirability of a husband and wife aiming at financial independence of each other after divorce, to the extent that this is realistic. Courts recognise, however, that women who have long been out of the job market cannot waltz straight back and, even if a job is found, it may well be with low earnings, little job security and few career prospects.

Generally speaking, a young woman with no children would be expected to go out to work. If there are very young children at home, a court would not expect a mother to go out to work unless she had been working before the breakdown of the marriage, in which case she would be expected to go on earning if practicable. This is also true of a father if the children live with him, except that it may be more realistic for him to go out to work, particularly if his level of earnings would mean that he could afford a housekeeper or childminder.

As the children grow older, the courts expect mothers to be able to return to work, at first perhaps part time, or after a period of re-training.

A woman who has not worked at all throughout the marriage, who has grown-up children and is herself only a few years from retirement age, is recognised as having a very limited earning capacity, perhaps none. The extent to which it might be reasonable to expect her to find paid employment would depend very much on how realistic an option this was, set against the background of the marriage, the husband's earnings, her health and all the other circumstances.

A woman who has not worked before, or not for a long time, may be disinclined to work now (especially if she feels her husband would then have more money to keep himself and his new companion). She would, however, have to justify why she could not be expected to work. Mere disinclination, or a determination to make her husband 'pay' for having left her, is not a valid objection.

The court cannot order anyone to get a job but it can 'deem' a wife a level of income which it considers she could earn, if it is felt she is simply refusing to get a job when she could reasonably do so. When working out what, if any, maintenance provision there should be, this deemed income is then included in the calculations as if it were income in her hands. Similarly, if a husband is thought to be deliberately keeping his earnings low, just to influence the maintenance claim, he can be deemed additional income of a level which the court considers he could realistically be earning and this is likewise included in calculating his obligations to his wife and family.

Part of the forward-looking emphasis of the 1984 Act is that the guidelines now specifically mention contributions to be made to the family's welfare in the foreseeable future (as well as those made in the past).

### conduct
The old provision was that the court had to take the conduct of each party into account 'so far as it was just to do so'. This was interpreted by the courts as meaning conduct which was 'really serious' or such that it would 'offend one's sense of justice not to take it into account'. The courts are now directed

to have regard to the conduct of each of the parties if that conduct is such that it would in the opinion of the court be inequitable to disregard it. Many lawyers and judges considered that the rewording of the statute simply put into clearer statutory form what the courts' practice already was, and there is little evidence to suggest a significant swing on the part of the courts as a result of the new wording of the guideline.

Conduct is only one of the factors to be taken into account. If it is suggested that the conduct of one party is such that it would be inequitable for the court to disregard it, the court must make a finding as to the seriousness of such conduct and must then decide how much weight is to be attached to the conduct in comparison with the other factors. It is, therefore, a two-stage test − first, is the conduct such that it would be inequitable for the court to disregard it, and second, how significant is such conduct in the light of all the other factors and, in particular, the needs and resources of the parties.

Courts are generally reluctant to decide that conduct is relevant because experience has shown that it is dangerous to make judgments about the cause of the breakdown of a marriage without full inquiry, since the conduct of one spouse can only be measured against the conduct of the other, and marriages seldom break down without faults on both sides.

The account taken of conduct may, with all the other circumstances, depend on the stage that the marriage reached, and whether there are children. For example, if a wife walked out on her husband after a very short period of marriage, little or no maintenance might be ordered but this would be due primarily to the fact that the marriage was very shortlived and without children rather than to 'conduct'.

With a marriage in its middle stage and with children, a wife's conduct is unlikely to have much influence on the financial settlement if to penalise her would mean penalising the children.

Although the applicant's conduct may be put forward as an argument for lower maintenance, the paying spouse's conduct can rarely be argued as a ground for increasing it, unless that spouse had done something (such as a serious criminal assault) that had affected the other's ability to earn a living.

**pension rights**
One factor the court has to consider is the possible loss by a divorced woman (or, less frequently, a man) of a right to a widow's pension under an occupational pension scheme of which the husband is a contributing member.

The trustees of a pension scheme have to abide by the rules of the scheme. These may allow discretion on the part of the trustees to decide who should get what. The rules may stipulate paying the widow's (or widower's) pension to the legal widow (or widower), and if there is no legal wife, a pension may be paid for the benefit of an orphan of the marriage or any adult dependant. A pension cannot normally be divided between a legal wife and an ex-wife. An orphan's right to a pension would not be lost on divorce, although it would be divided between the orphans of the first and any subsequent marriage.

Although an ex-wife cannot claim any share of a widow's pension, she could try to claim a dependant's benefit or (perhaps part of) the scheme's lump sum benefit. Occupational pension schemes normally include a lump sum death benefit of up to four times' a member's pay on his death before retirement. The trustees would normally take into account the member's wishes in the 'expression of wish' form which he will have completed when he joined the scheme. (A scheme member can at any time alter his nomination of whom he wishes to get the lump sum.) On the death of the divorced husband, the trustees may be able to use their discretion where appropriate to divide the lump sum between the ex-wife and any current legal wife or cohabitant.

Many pension schemes provide that on the death of a member after retirement, the widow will be entitled to perhaps one half of the pension prospectively due to be received by her late husband. Under the majority of pension schemes, a divorced former spouse is not likely to be eligible.

Some pension schemes may allow a member to give up part of his own pension at retirement to provide in return a pension for his ex-spouse after his death.

The court can try to have the wife compensated for loss of what her pension entitlement would be. It cannot order the husband to take out life insurance or an annuity, but it can order the husband to provide capital by way of a lump sum to enable her to buy a deferred annuity for that amount, to start at his death or at retirement age and to continue until her death.

An alternative solution is to increase the wife's share in the matrimonial home by way of compensating her for the loss of pension rights.

Where the divorce is based on separation and the court is asked to consider what the respondent's financial position will be after divorce, the court may refuse to allow the decree to be made absolute unless and until a satisfactory insurance policy has been taken out to be vested in the wife.

### new companion

If either or both of you have formed a new relationship, this may make the break-up of your marriage less financially damaging. The fact that the other is moving out to live with somebody else, although emotionally hurtful, may be the best thing that could happen as far as accommodation costs are concerned. It reduces the biggest financial strain of all – two sets of accommodation costs from one income.

Where an ex-spouse's living expenses and accommodation costs are substantially reduced because of a new partner's contribution, there is more of the ex-spouses' money to go around and be shared out.

Where a spouse has taken on new liabilities to a new wife or husband or cohabitant, the court takes those liabilities into account when considering the maintenance order, while trying not to reduce the ex-spouse's standard of living to below that of the new spouse.

Basically, the new spouse cannot be required to contribute towards support for the previous spouse and family – but her or his means are taken into account in deciding the paying ex-spouse's liabilities.

In order to be satisfied that the full picture of contribution has been revealed, the new partner's means usually come under review of the court. He or she cannot be forced to produce an affidavit of means but can be summoned to court and be questioned as to his or her means. The court does not necessarily require to know what a new wife or cohabitant earns, but will want to know the extent to which she relieves the ex-husband from having to provide for her – and also for himself.

### length of the marriage
Whether a period of time living together before marriage is taken into account will depend on all the circumstances. It is likely to be taken into account if children were born during that period, or if one party had made a substantial financial contribution to the shared home before marriage.

After a short marriage and where there are no children, the court may be inclined not to order maintenance, or perhaps only for a limited period. A short marriage between a young couple who are both working or able to do so is likely to be treated very differently from a short marriage between two people in, say, their mid-fifties where the woman had given up secure accommodation and/or a career and/or maintenance from a former spouse when she married.

## clean break

The court has the explicit obligation when making an order for financial relief, to consider whether it would be appropriate to make an order so that each spouse would become financially independent of the other 'as soon after the grant of the decree as the court considers just and reasonable'.

This is a specific statutory recognition of what was already a groundswell of support for the 'clean break' principle. The wording of the 1984 Act does not, however, say that a clean break is inevitably desirable, nor say that if there is to be a clean break it must always take immediate effect. On the contrary, the court has first to consider whether a clean break approach is appropriate and then, if it is, when and how that approach should be implemented, paying heed to what is just and reasonable in the circumstances.

Where an order for periodical payments is to be made to a spouse and a clean break is appropriate, the court should consider whether the payments should be only for a specific period. The specified period should be what in the opinion of the court would be sufficient to enable the recipient spouse to adjust without undue hardship to the ending of his or her financial dependence on the other spouse. In practice, courts are reluctant to look more than two to three years into the future and only if the future is pretty clearly foreseeable will a limited term order be appropriate. Time-limited periodical payments are much less likely to be appropriate where there are dependent children than, say, where there has been a short childless marriage and what the wife requires is just one or two years of financial assistance while she re-establishes herself.

A clean-break settlement is sometimes fair and reasonable, not on the basis of time-limited maintenance but by one spouse 'buying out' the other's maintenance claims with an additional capital payment. The court will look at all the circumstances, including the wife's prospects of remarriage and any future earning capacity. The availability of funds (or, more usually, their non-availability) is critical.

Even in those rare cases where there are ample funds, the capital awarded is unlikely to be enough to produce, when invested, as high an annual return at standard interest rates as the maintenance provision there might otherwise have been. Moreover, the lump sum cannot later be increased to keep pace with inflation or a husband's financial fortune. The husband for his part might well feel indignant if his wife remarries a few years later.

Even if there is no capital other than the net equity of the matrimonial home, a couple may prefer the wife to receive all or a disproportionate part of the net equity and to have her maintenance claims dismissed. But this is not always a realistic solution and must be considered very carefully.

Before the 1984 Act, the courts had effectively already been able to order virtual clean break settlements by refusing to order more than nominal periodical payments if circumstances so warranted but a claim for maintenance could not be finally dismissed without the applicant's consent. The 1984 Act has given the courts more muscle: where a clean break approach is appropriate, a spouse's maintenance claim can now be dismissed either at once or by an order for maintenance for only a specific period. Also, a court order can now be made to prevent one spouse from having a claim on the estate of the other spouse under the Inheritance (Provision for Family and Dependants) Act 1975.

Courts have a duty to investigate whether it is realistic to expect a husband and wife to be moving towards financial independence, but where there are dependent children, this may very well not be in their interests, and the courts have a specific duty to give first consideration to the welfare of children. In any case, the clean break approach can extend only to the parties to the marriage, not to provision for children.

## guidelines on maintenance levels

The court's overall task is to evaluate all the various factors, balance the factors one against the other, giving what weight it considers appropriate to each factor, and then try to arrive at an order which is fair and reasonable.

In the majority of cases, the court is primarily concerned to see to what extent the needs of the wife and children, in so far as they are not met by her own resources, can be met out of the resources of the husband. Frequently, there just is not enough money available to do this and the court then merely orders the husband to pay what he can reasonably be expected to afford, leaving the wife to look to supplementary benefit or family income supplement to meet her needs.

There is no such thing as set rates for maintenance to be paid to a spouse. The couple's finances, both income and capital, are looked at in the light of the guidelines laid down by statute. The way the courts apply their guidelines is – and must be – flexible to meet particular needs. What the court can do in any case is largely limited by the resources available to the particular couple.

The court will look to see what a wife's reasonable needs are and how these needs could be met – by her own earning capacity, her husband's earning capacity or a combination of the two. Capital and income are looked at together. It may be appropriate for a wife to receive more capital and less maintenance even if there is not to be a clean break.

Where there is more money available, the aim of the court is to share this out as fairly as possible between the parties, taking into account their respective needs to provide a home and for food and clothing. A traditional approach, which is still quite often used in middle income cases, is the one-third starting point. This is calculated by adding together both parties' incomes and working out what level of maintenance would be required to bring the applicant's gross income up to one-third of the combined gross incomes. The court may then work out what the impact of tax would be for each party, producing a 'net effect'. The net effect is what income you would each be left with if the one-third formula were applied, taking children's maintenance payments into account. This is then generally compared with what each spouse's reasonable needs are. The one-third starting point, the net effect formula and consideration of both parties' needs are methods of approach, not hard and fast rules.

The attitude of the courts towards what is appropriate by way of provision for children of the family is generally a rather less complicated calculation: children's maintenance orders fall within a more standardised bracket.

**orders for the children**
In making financial orders for children, the court will have regard to the child's financial needs, earning capacity, property and income and also the manner in which the parents had planned for him or her to be educated or trained.

The court has power to make orders in respect of any 'child of the family'. This is defined as not only a child of both of you (which includes an adopted child) but also any other whom you have treated as a child of your family (except foster children).

You could be ordered to make payments for your spouse's children from a former marriage or relationship, provided you had treated them as your children. This liability to maintain is, however, mitigated by the fact that the court is required to consider the liability of any other person to maintain them (for example, their natural parent) and whether, when treating them as your children, you thought they were your own and now you find that they were the result of an adulterous relationship of which you were unaware.

Orders in favour of children requested in the petition can be any of the ones that can be made for a wife or husband. In practice, it is very unusual for the court to do other than order periodical payments for a child.

There may be a separate, earlier hearing to order maintenance for the children, before the main financial hearing.

An order for payments to children comes into effect as soon as it is made, even if this is before the decree. The order can be backdated to the date when the application was made, If made by the petitioner, this means the date the petition was filed; if by the respondent, the date he or she issued the notice of application for maintenance.

Unless the court otherwise provides, an order will not continue beyond the child's 17th birthday (i.e. the one following compulsory school leaving age). But the court has power to make an order to remain in force up to the child's 18th birthday while the child is in full-time education or for longer if there are other special circumstances – for example, disability.

There are no universally accepted guidelines about the financial needs of children. The task of the court is to establish what is the reasonable cost of maintaining the children in the circumstances of the particular parents.

To avoid detailed and often unrealistic enquiry, registrars have certain basic guidelines. The lowest common denominators are the DHSS allowances for calculating supplementary benefit, which are at present (until April 1988):

| | |
|---|---|
| child under 11 | £10.40 per week |
| child aged 11–15 | £15.60 per week |
| child of 16 or 17 | £18.75 per week |

A registrar may use these figures as a guide, multiplied according to the husband's income. In most cases, however, the significant factor is not so much the husband's income as the number of children.

The DHSS figures provide for little more than bare essentials, and where there is more money available, the foster parent allowance being paid by the local authority will be a more realistic assessment of the cost of maintaining children. Foster parent basic rates (exclusive of holiday and birthday allowances) recommended by the National Foster Care Association in 1987, are:

| child aged | | |
|---|---|---|
| 0–4 | £28.98 per week |
| 5–7 | £33.81 per week |
| 8–10 | £37.03 per week |
| 11–12 | £40.32 per week |
| 13–15 | £43.54 per week |
| 16–18 | £58.03 per week |

(for London, the recommended rate is 11% higher).

Foster parents are not entitled to child benefit, and this should be deducted from these figures. Registrars take into account the fact that child benefit (at present £7.25 per week per child, plus a payment of £4.70 if a single parent) will be paid to whichever parent has the children living with him or her. Child benefit may be counted in as part of the parent's resources or, more often, it is treated as a contribution towards the cost of maintaining the child or children. The registrar may use either (or neither) of these approaches in his calculations.

## the registrar's decision

The registrar is likely to give judgment there and then, once all the evidence and all the arguments have been heard, or judgment may be reserved to a later date.

If the registrar dismisses an application for periodical payments, it cannot later be revived. The applicant may have agreed to this in return for some other financial provision, such as a larger lump sum or transfer of the home.

Make a written note of the registrar's judgment in case there should be an appeal. It may also be useful to have a note of the registrar's basis for arriving at the payments ordered – for instance, his reasons for departing from the one-third starting point, or a low maintenance payment because the wife receives a larger share in the matrimonial home. This may be taken into account on any subsequent application to vary a periodical payments order.

An order for costs to be paid can be asked for at this stage, as soon as the registrar has given his decision. You will have to explain why you think an order for costs should be made (or why there should be no order) and produce the relevant figures of overall costs incurred. This is the time to raise the question of any costs 'reserved' on a previous interim application which deferred the decision on the amount of costs until the final financial order.

After the hearing, the court office prepares the order(s) and sends a copy to both parties. Check the wording and figures carefully, in case there is a clerical error. Then keep the documents in a safe place.

If any orders will affect your tax position (which is likely), a further copy should be sent to your inspector of taxes as promptly as possible, together with a copy of the application that led to the order.

### *appeal*
An appeal against an order or decision of the registrar can be made to a judge by filing a notice of appeal within five working days. The notice setting out the grounds is best prepared by a solicitor.

### 'registering' the order

It is possible to apply to the registrar for the order for maintenance to be registered in the magistrates' court of the area
where you live or work. The purpose is to make enforcement
simpler.

A statement in a prescribed form (N.113, obtainable from the
county court) including the names and addresses of the parties
and the amount of maintenance payable, must be lodged at the
divorce court and a fee paid (at present, £2).

The maintenance order is sent to the magistrates' court and
the payer then has to make all payments through that court,
which keeps a record of them. If the payer has fallen into
arrears, the payee can request the clerk to the justices to take
the necessary steps to enforce the order.

Enforcement can include distraint upon goods, attachment
of earnings, and (as a last resort) imprisonment for up to six
weeks.

An order registered at the magistrates' court can be assigned
to the DHSS and if the payer falls into arrears, the recipient can
get supplementary benefit instead, if eligible.

When an order is registered, either party can apply to the
magistrates' court (instead of the divorce court) to vary the
order, or the payer can apply there to be let off any arrears.

# TAX AND MAINTENANCE PAYMENTS

The rates of income tax for the 1987/88 tax year are:

|  | £ £ | % |
|---|---|---|
| on taxable income of | 0 – 17,900 | 27 |
| *plus* on taxable income of | 17,901 – 20,400 | 40 |
|  | 20,401 – 25,400 | 45 |
|  | 25,401 – 33,300 | 50 |
|  | 33,301 – 41,200 | 55 |
|  | above 41,200 | 60 |

Taxable income is the income remaining after deducting certain payments, such as occupational pension contributions, maintenance payments made under a court order, and taking off personal tax allowances.

While a couple are still married, all their income is deemed to be the husband's for tax purposes (unless they have applied to be separately taxed).

From the date of separation, each spouse is taxed separately on his or her own income. The key point to remember is that it is the date of separation which is critical, not the date of divorce.

The law provides that a married couple are to be treated as living together unless

○ they are separated by court order, deed of separation or separation agreement (and are living apart)

or

○ they are in fact separated in such circumstances that the separation is likely to be permanent.

**personal tax allowances**
A set amount of every person's annual income is not taxed. Most of these personal allowances change each tax year (which runs from 6 April to 5 April).

For the tax year 1987/88, the following are the personal tax allowances.

*single person's personal allowance – £2,425*
available to single adults and to children, also to anyone separated or divorced and not remarried. This is available in full to a wife to use against her own income arising in the remainder of the tax year of separation (and every subsequent tax year unless and until she marries again).

*married man's personal allowance – £3,795*
available to a married man who is residing with his wife or who is separated and is wholly maintaining her by payments made voluntarily (if paying maintenance to his wife under an enforceable agreement or court order, he gets the single person's allowance).

He continues to get this allowance for the remainder of the tax year in which he separates or gets divorced. If he marries again, he gets this allowance on the basis of his second marriage.

*wife's earned income allowance – £2,425 or amount of earned income whichever is lower*
available only to a married man whose wife has an income from employment or self-employment. A husband is given wife's earned income allowance in full on his wife's earnings for the period up to separation.

*lone parent's additional personal allowance (APA) – £1,370*
can be claimed by a mother or a father, whether separated or divorced, if she or he is eligible for the single person's allowance and has a 'qualifying' child living with her or him for the whole or any part of the tax year.

The definition of a qualifying child is a complicated one. Basically, you need to show

i) that you are the natural parent or step-parent or have adopted the child
*and*
ii) that the child was under 16 at the start of the current tax year.

You may, however, still claim for children who are between 16 and 18, if they are receiving full-time instruction at a university, college, school or other educational establishment, or undergoing training for a trade or vocation for the minimum of a two-year period.

This allowance is the same whether there is just one child, or any number of children. If the child lives partly with the father and partly with the mother in any one year, the allowance may be divided proportionately or claimed by just one parent. Bear this in mind when working out the net effect of financial proposals. Where there are several children, and some live with one parent, some with the other, both parents can claim the full additional personal allowance.

A father will not get the additional personal allowance during a tax year in which he is still getting the married man's allowance.

Details of all the personal allowances are given in Inland Revenue leaflet IR22; leaflet IR29 deals with income tax and one-parent families and IR30 with separation and divorce.

### example: *separation and personal tax allowances*
Husband and wife are both working, and he has been paying the tax due on both their incomes less the married man's personal tax allowance and wife's earned income allowance.

On November 5, their marriage having broken down, they separate. In order to calculate tax liability in these circumstances, the wife's income has to be apportioned into what she earned in the months of the tax year prior to separation and what she has earned afterwards. She is entitled to the single person's allowance in full to set against income she earns in the remaining 5 months of the tax year after the separation. The husband is entitled to his married man's allowance for the whole of the tax year and for wife's earned income relief on money earned by the wife in the 7 months of the tax year before the separation.

In the tax year of separation, the husband and the wife pay less tax between them than if they had remained together. This is because she has the single person's allowance for the full year to set against her income after separation. (All things being equal, it probably makes sense from the tax point of view for the date of separation to be earlier rather than late in the tax year.)

In the following years of separation, the couple will be taxed like any two single people.

*action to take*
The wife must notify her tax office as soon as the separation is going to be permanent, otherwise she will end up paying too much tax. Assuming that she is taxed on a PAYE basis, her notice of coding for the year will have taken into account wife's earned income allowance. She must get her coding altered as soon as possible, or alternatively has to make a tax repayment claim at the end of the year.

## on break-up of a marriage

When you are splitting up or when you are getting divorced, it is essential that you arrange maintenance payments in such a way as to minimise tax as much as possible.

### if voluntary payment
Where maintenance is paid voluntarily rather than under a court order or an enforceable agreement, it remains the payer's income for tax purposes (i.e. has to be paid out of taxed income). But the recipient does not have to pay tax on it.

### if payment by court order or agreement

Where maintenance is paid either under an enforceable maintenance agreement or subject to a court order, the amount of the payment ceases to be counted as the payer's income and becomes the recipient's income for tax purposes. The tax is 'collected' for the Inland Revenue by the payer, who deducts tax at the standard rate (27% for 1987/88) from the payments that he makes. In other words, the maintenance has the tax taken off before it ever reaches the recipient's hands. If she is not liable to pay any tax, she can reclaim tax deducted up to her personal allowance, but getting it may cause serious cash-flow problems for her.

*example: **paying maintenance and tax***
The wife was not earning when they split up and the only one with income is the husband (£8,000). He decides he will pay her £2,500 per annum voluntarily:

|                                      |   £   |
|--------------------------------------|------:|
|                                      |   £   |
| H's total income                     | 8,000 |
| *less*: single person's tax allowance | 2,425 |
| H's taxable income                   | 5,575 |

    H pays tax at 27% on £5,575 = £1,505
    H has (£8,000 − £1,505 − £2,500) = £4,095
    W receives £2,500 tax free.
    H, therefore, has to find £2,500 out of his income after he has paid tax whereas W has no tax burden at all. H is left with less than half his gross income.

If the same amount of maintenance were paid under a court order, the position would be:

|                                      |       |   £   |
|--------------------------------------|------:|------:|
| H's total income                     |       | 8,000 |
| *less:* single person's tax allowance | 2,425 |       |
| maintenance for W                    | 2,500 |       |
|                                      | 4,925 |       |
| H's taxable income                   |       | 3,075 |

| H pays tax | £ |
|---|---|
| on own taxable income at 27% | 830 |
| on behalf of W's maintenance | |
| at 27% on £2,500 | 675 |
| | 1,505 |

H has (£8,000 − £1,505 − £1,825) = £4,670

H pays only £1,825 to W and the Inland Revenue gets the £675 tax on her maintenance from him during the year through his PAYE.

(If the person deducting the tax is on schedule E – which people working for an employer normally are – his PAYE code number will remain unaltered. If, on the other hand, he is self-employed, he would have to include details of the retained tax in his tax return and the Inland Revenue will raise a separate assessment under schedule D (iii).)

The £2,500 maintenance is now subject to tax in W's hands as follows:

| | £ |
|---|---|
| W's total income (maintenance from H) | 2,500 |
| *less:* single person's tax allowance | 2,425 |
| W's taxable income | 75 |

Her liability for tax at 27% on £75 is £20. But H has deducted £675 tax over the year when paying her. She has therefore suffered too much tax and must reclaim from the Inland Revenue £655 (£675 − £20) overpaid tax.

Husband and wife between them pay £655 less tax than they would if he paid her voluntarily, because the wife's single person's tax allowance has been utilised. The husband does much better out of this than the wife. In addition, her cash-flow situation is worse: during the year, she received only £1,825 from him and is then left to claim the balance from the Inland Revenue.

**reclaiming tax**

The husband should supply a 'certificate of deduction of tax' (form R.185) with each payment or at regular, agreed, intervals throughout the year. The wife has to forward these to her tax office with her own claim form R249 (for monthly or quarterly claims) or R40 (for claiming at the end of the financial year) in order to get back the balance from the Inland Revenue. She may not get the money due to her until some considerable time afterwards, at least not until her original claim has been processed and a routine established. And if the husband fails to produce form R.185, this causes problems and delay over recovery of the tax.

Most tax inspectors deal with tax repayment claims quarterly, some are prepared to do so monthly. Get in touch with your tax inspector as soon as possible and ask what will happen in your case. Some tax offices will not consider a tax repayment claim until the tax return has been filed, so make sure that you complete your tax return promptly.

Cash-flow is a problem mainly during the first months of payments, because subsequently there will be the booster of the tax refund from the previous period. This could be seen as a form of compulsory saving, but a disadvantageous one (particularly if inflation is high).

**changing from voluntary payments**

A woman may well be getting substantially less in hand when her husband switches over from voluntary maintenance to paying maintenance under a court order, leaving her with the responsibility of making a tax repayment claim. This may be exacerbated if voluntary maintenance was paid in advance and the order is payable in arrears. On the other hand, a husband may not realise that if he is required to pay under a court order the same gross amount that he was paying voluntarily, he is going to have more cash in hand to the extent of 27% of whatever amount he is paying under an order.

It is important to work out the tax effect of an order, particularly when it involves a switch from voluntary payments to payments under an order for the first time. For example, in 1987/88 the payer could raise the gross amount by 36.9% when switching to a court order, and this would leave him in the same net position as before. A recipient would also be in exactly the same net position if she had other income which swallowed up her tax allowance, but if she had no other income, she would gain because her single person's tax allowance would be utilised.

### backdated orders
Where a court order for maintenance provides for payments to be made for a period before the date of the order, the Inland Revenue may accept that such payments can be taken into account for tax purposes provided that

o payments do not relate to a period before the date of the application for the order
o the parties agree
o there has been no undue delay by the parties in pressing the application.

## small maintenance payments

Where there is a court order of around £2,500, it may be better for the ordered payment to be reduced slightly to make it come within the statutory provisions for 'small maintenance payments'.

Maintenance payable to a spouse under a court order that does not exceed £48 a week or £208 a month is treated for tax purposes as a 'small maintenance payment' and will be paid gross. No certificates of deduction of income tax are then supplied or needed. To qualify as a small maintenance payment, the amount ordered must be expressed as payable 'per month' or 'per week', not annually. (Payments made by a voluntary arrangement cannot be treated as small maintenance payments.)

Small maintenance limits are important where the wife cannot afford to wait to get tax repayments and cannot be certain that the husband will provide tax deduction certificates (form R.185).

The amount of tax which is payable does not alter, only its method of collection:

○ the payer does not deduct tax at source but makes each payment gross
○ the payer's own PAYE code number will be altered, in order to make up for this
○ the recipient, instead of having tax deducted at source, fills in a tax return at the end of the year and will then be assessed for tax. Thus, her cash-flow position is considerably improved.

In order to ensure that he does not pay too much tax, the payer must tell his tax office as soon as payment under the order begins so that the fact that his taxable income has been reduced can be noted and his notice of coding altered. (The higher the code number, the less tax you pay.)

The recipient gets the maintenance payments in full and does not have to pay tax on them until later. For a recipient whose only tax allowance is the single person's allowance (£2,425), there will be tax due on the amount between that and the maximum small maintenance payment (£2,496 a year). If she is in employment and paid under PAYE, Inland Revenue will collect the tax due by altering her notice of coding for the following tax year. But if she is not in the PAYE scheme, a problem can arise if she does not realise that the maintenance is taxable. Small maintenance payments can pile up tax liability when the recipient does not know that she is supposed to include them in her tax return and pay tax on them – and then, three or four years later, is faced with a massive claim for unpaid tax.

*example*

In the example given on pages 147–148, if the maintenance were reduced by £5, it would just fall within the 'small maintenance payments' bracket and therefore be paid gross – but still taxable in the wife's hands.

|  |  | £ |
|---|---|---|
| H's taxable income | | 3,080 |
| H pays | | |
| tax on own income | 831 | |
| gross maintenance to W | 2,495 | |
| | | 3,326 |

from his total income of £8,000, H is left with £4,674
W receives £2,495
her personal tax allowance is £2,425
her taxable income is £70
so her tax liability is £18.90.

She must not forget to account to the Inland Revenue for this: otherwise the Revenue, when it discovers the position, could insist on payments that have accrued in past 'forgotten' years.

## where there are children

Basically, children are treated in the same way for tax purposes as the spouse. But the paying parent should

o always make maintenance payments under a court order – payments by a voluntary arrangement (or even under a legally binding agreement) are not tax effective

o always express the maintenance to be payable 'to the child' – not to the other parent 'for the child' or 'for the child's benefit'.

Provided these arrangements are followed, maintenance paid to the child will be treated as his or her income for tax purposes. Accordingly, the child's own single person's tax allowance can be set against it so that £2,425 a year (1987/88) is free of tax. Whereas if the order were for payment to the mother for the child, the payments for the child would count as hers for tax purposes. It is not necessary to open a special trust fund or bank account for the children. The mother can receive the money on their behalf as 'agent'. The important thing for the Inland Revenue is that the order is worded 'to the children' and not 'to the mother for the children'.

An order normally ceases when the child becomes 17, but can be made to continue until a specified event. But unless this is made clear in the order by wording such as "until the child attains the age of 17 years or ceases full-time education (whichever is the later) . . .", the Inland Revenue may not allow tax relief on payments after the age of 17.

If the father wants to pay for the children at a fee-paying school, payment of the fees can be arranged in a tax advantageous way. Provided the father has no contractual liability himself to the school, he could increase the amount of the net maintenance the child will receive to cover school fees, and the mother, on behalf of the child, would pay the bills from the maintenance. He can only get tax relief on fees he pays direct to the school if there is a contract in a form specifically approved by the Inland Revenue between the child and the school. Because of the precision that is needed in drafting effective documents, it is advisable to consult a solicitor if you pay for private schooling for your children.

### small maintenance payments for children
If an order for payment to a child is for a sum that does not exceed £48 a week or £208 a month, the payment counts as small maintenance and payments are made gross. For payments made to a spouse for the benefit of a child rather than to a child direct, the small maintenance limit is £25 a week or £108 a month.

For small maintenance payments, the age limit for 'child' is 21 years.

If a court order specifies a certain amount for a spouse and certain amounts for each child, each amount is treated as a separate maintenance payment. So, for example, if a court orders £30 per week to be paid to a wife for herself and £30 to her for her child, the first will be treated as a small maintenance payment (because it is below £48 a week) and be paid gross, whereas the second will be treated as a 'large' maintenance payment (because it is above £25 a week for a child) and will be paid net of tax – the payer deducting 27% before making the payment.

### children's personal tax allowances
The court order should be arranged to make use of the available personal tax allowances. For example, a separated wife and two small children have, between them, combined personal allowances of £8,645 namely:

|                                                      | £     |
| ---------------------------------------------------- | ----- |
| wife: single person's allowance                      | 2,425 |
| additional personal allowance for lone parent (APA)  | 1,370 |
| 1st child: single person's allowance                 | 2,425 |
| 2nd child: single person's allowance                 | 2,425 |
|                                                      | 8,645 |

Therefore, if the husband were to submit to a court order for periodical payments of £3,795 a year to the wife and £2,425 a year to each child of the family, the wife and the children would receive £8,645 a year tax free provided that they had no other taxable income. At the same time, the husband would be able to claim tax relief on the £8,645 he paid because it would not be regarded as his income for tax purposes.

Child benefit also is not taxable. In 1987/88, child benefit for a single parent with two children comes to £998.40 a year. She can therefore receive £9,643.40 in the year without having to pay any tax on it. But she has to reclaim from the Inland Revenue the tax deducted by the husband from the maintenance payments to her.

It might be argued that the order in the example is slightly artificial in that it makes the maintenance for the children disproportionately high. There is a potential drawback in such an order for the husband or for the wife.

From the husband's point of view, if he were to agree to an order with such high payments to the children and the wife were then to remarry, he might find it difficult when applying for a variation in the order for the children's maintenance to convince the court that the orders for the children should now be reduced by a substantial downward variation because, prior to the ex-wife's remarriage, they were at a disproportionately high level in order to save tax.

From the wife's point of view, if she agrees to higher maintenance for the children and lower for herself for these reasons, when maintenance payments for older children cease, her own maintenance would be at an unrealistically low level.

It would, therefore, be prudent to ensure that the registrar makes a note that the high maintenance for the children was agreed to relieve the wife of tax, in case she wishes to apply for an increase or the ex-husband wishes to apply for a downward variation. Where there is a consent order, an exchange of correspondence confirming the reasons for the high maintenance for the children would be helpful. You could also record in such a note how you agree the payments would have been divided between the wife and the children if it were not for tax considerations. This will serve as a guide if you later seek a variation, perhaps on the wife's remarriage or as children's payments cease.

Although it is quite lawful to arrange your affairs so as to minimise tax liabilities, there is always a risk that the Inland Revenue will decide that you have overstepped the boundary and that the form of the order is a sham, solely for gaining tax relief. This is an increasingly grey area – if in doubt, consult a solicitor first.

## maintenance and higher rate taxpayers

Where the person who is paying maintenance earns a sufficiently high income to come within the higher tax rates, the potential tax saving is even greater. Since the whole of the maintenance payment is set against his income (in addition to his personal tax allowance), the payer's taxable income may be brought down to a lower tax band. Because maintenance paid under a court order ceases to be counted as the payer's income for tax purposes, income that would be taxed in the payer's hands at, for example, 50%, when it becomes the income of the ex-wife or children is likely to attract either no tax or only the standard rate of 27%.

## making tax arrangements

Understanding how income tax works enables you to save as much income tax as possible through the proper organisation of maintenance orders.

The golden rules are

- agree the date on which you separated, for tax purposes
- do not pay maintenance voluntarily for longer than necessary
- make an enforceable agreement or get a court order at the earliest possible stage
- where there are children, get court orders directing payments to them as soon as possible
- if paying maintenance towards the upkeep of children, spread the money between ex-spouse and children in such a way as to take maximum advantage of their respective personal tax allowances (keep a clear acknowledgment signed by both of you that this is what has been done)
- make children's periodical payments payable to the child and not to the ex-spouse 'for the child's benefit'
- where appropriate, make use of the small maintenance payments provisions to avoid cash-flow problems for the recipient.

# THE MATRIMONIAL HOME

The expression 'the matrimonial home' is used in the context of divorce to refer to the home – house or flat – acquired by husband or wife or both to be lived in by the family during their joint lives.

There are basically three kinds of order that the divorce court makes:

○ for a sale, with division of the proceeds
○ for transfer of one spouse's interest to the other
○ for a postponed sale – usually until the children complete their education but sometimes beyond that, the house then to be sold and the proceeds divided in specified proportions.

There are no laid-down principles as to when the court will make one or other of these orders or in what proportion it will order the proceeds of sale to be split. A sale and 50/50 division of the proceeds will be appropriate in many cases, but there are many others where this would operate unfairly against one or other of the parties. The court's decision in each case largely depends on whether there are any children, the age of the parties, the length of the marriage and whether the spouse who will move out has potentially secure accommodation.

## rented property

The divorce court has power to make a transfer of tenancy order on divorce with regard to any tenancy – private or local authority.

Many leases contain a clause that the tenancy should not be assigned without the landlord's consent. But the law provides that such consent should not be unreasonably withheld and if the court were to make a transfer order and the landlord objected, this would probably be evidence of withholding consent unreasonably. It would be wiser to obtain the landlord's consent, preferably in writing, before an application for transfer of the tenancy is made.

### protected tenancy
Where a tenancy is a 'protected' tenancy (within the Rent Act 1977), the court can order it to be transferred to the other spouse under the Matrimonial Causes Act 1973, just like any other property. Application can be made at decree nisi and an order will take effect on decree absolute.

### statutory tenancy
Where a protected tenancy has become a 'statutory' tenancy (for example, because the landlord has served notice to quit on the occupying tenant – the husband or the wife or both of them), the tenant has a right to remain on the premises unless and until the landlord can obtain a possession order.

Although there would no longer be any 'property' in the understood sense, the wife (assuming the tenancy is in the husband's name) may still be able to obtain a transfer to her of the statutory tenancy under the Matrimonial Homes Act 1983 (in which case, notice has to be given to the landlord). It is vital, however, that the tenancy should be transferred before decree absolute because, once she is no longer the wife and the husband has left home, there will be no tenant in occupation within the meaning of the Act and thus the statutory tenancy will have lapsed.

### council tenancy
Any such tenancy is 'property' and can be transferred under the Matrimonial Causes Act as part of the financial arrangements on divorce (also under the Matrimonial Homes Act). It is not possible simply to ask the local authority to adjust the tenancy (as used to be the case before the 1980 Housing Act).

Local authorities are more or less in the same position as private landlords when it comes to obtaining possession and if, for example, the house is in the husband's name, the local authority cannot merely serve notice to quit on the husband and give a new tenancy to the wife.

# owner-occupied property

If the property is in joint names and expressed on the title deeds to be for the benefit of both parties equally, each has a half share in the 'net equity', whatever the respective contributions. If it is simply in both names, without this further statement dealing with the division of the 'equity', the co-owners' respective shares will not necessarily be equal.

Although the court needs to assess what the financial interest of husband and wife is in the home, in most cases this is only the first stage of the process by which the court decides what is to happen.

Whose name the house is actually in – husband's, wife's or jointly – and who put up the deposit and who paid the mortgage are obviously important but by no means the decisive factors when sharing out on divorce.

## where there are no children

On divorce after a short marriage, the court may look mainly at financial contributions and decide that the person who put the most in should have the most out. But the longer the marriage has gone on, the less the court is interested in who put in what, in money terms, and the more it is prepared to recognise the other party's non-money contribution. For instance, the wife's contribution in keeping the home going may count as much as the husband's financial contributions.

The main consideration is likely to be whether the net proceeds of sale of the house are likely to be sufficient to enable each spouse (with the aid of such mortgage loan as each might reasonably be expected to obtain) to buy an adequate new home. If so, the court may well order a sale without delay. Even if one of them wants to stay on, it may not be practicable or fair to the other for him or her to do so. The house may have to be sold where the combined resources of husband and wife are insufficient to keep up the mortgage repayments on the existing home and to provide accommodation for the other spouse.

Where the home had been bought from the local authority with a discounted mortgage and it is sold within 3 years of buying, you have to pay back to the local authority part of the discount you were allowed. This may well be an argument for asking the court to defer a sale until the 3-year period is up.

### share in the proceeds
The court will take into account direct financial contributions by the non-owning spouse towards the purchase (payment of part of the deposit or part of the mortgage repayments) or for the improvement of the house. It will also consider indirect financial contributions – for example, where the wife has worked for all or part of the marriage and has used her earnings to pay some of the household bills, food, clothing or has paid her earnings into the couple's joint bank account.

If the wife's share would be insufficient to enable her to buy a new home, particularly if her earning capacity puts her into a less favourable position for getting a mortgage, the court could order that the wife should get a greater share of the proceeds of sale. The court may compensate the husband by ordering him to pay relatively low maintenance to the wife – or none at all.

### not selling
A sale of the matrimonial home may, however, not be the right solution. The expenses of selling, and of buying two other houses, will have to be met, and the net proceeds of sale may not be sufficient to enable either spouse to buy another home.

(Moreover, if either party was legally aided, the Law Society may claim part of the proceeds for the legal aid fund's statutory charge.)

The court could order that the wife remain in the house

○ until she wants to move out, or marries again, or cohabits (this is normally taken to be the case after, say, 6 months of living together, but preferably should be defined in the order) or she dies

or

○ for a period of time specified by the court.

The house would then be sold, and the net proceeds divided in the proportions decided by the court at the time of making the order (these cannot be varied later).

If she is not making the mortgage payments, the wife might be ordered to pay to the husband in the meantime something in the way of rent in respect of the husband's half (or other share) of the house. In practice, this might be achieved by an appropriate reduction of his maintenance obligations to her.

An arrangement which leaves the wife with a degree of uncertainty as to her future home, and the husband having to wait a number of years to receive his capital while he has to continue paying maintenance, can cause bitterness. The courts try to avoid some of these difficulties by arranging a 'clean break': for example, it might be fair for the house to be transferred outright to the wife and the husband compensated by the wife's claim for maintenance being dismissed.

If an order is made for the transfer of the whole of the home into the other spouse's name or from one into the joint names, a transfer or conveyance will have to be drawn up. On the transfer of property by court order following the break-up of a marriage, irrespective of the value of the property, stamp duty is not payable. Where a solicitor is required for the convey-ancing, the work can be done under the green form scheme or a legal aid certificate.

*buying out the other spouse*

An alternative 'clean break' arrangement is for the spouse who is going to remain in the house to buy out the departing spouse, by paying him or her a lump sum for his or her share in the house. If this is done by the remaining spouse borrowing the money or raising an extra mortgage, there will be tax relief on the interest.

If the person who has been bought out uses the money towards buying another house and borrows the rest on mortgage, he or she will get tax relief on the interest on a loan of up to £30,000. In other words, both spouses can take advantage of the full amount of tax relief on mortgages for a house each.

## where there are children

The court's priority is that an adequate home should be provided for the children.

### selling

It is unlikely that the court would order a sale unless selling the home would bring in enough money to buy other adequate accommodation for the parent who is going to have the children (usually the wife) to live there with them.

The house would, however, have to be sold if the wife could not keep up the mortgage repayments with whatever assistance by way of maintenance the husband could finance. More economical accommodation would then have to be bought for her and the children out of the proceeds of selling the house.

### not selling

To secure the house as a home for the children, the court may order the husband to transfer it into joint names if it has been in his sole name. When a house is in joint names, it cannot normally be sold without the agreement of the joint owners, but either party can apply to the High Court for an order to enforce a sale. To prevent this, the divorce court normally directs that the house shall not be sold for a specific period while she and the children live there – usually until the youngest child reaches school-leaving age.

An alternative is to transfer the house into the wife's sole name subject to a charge securing to the husband whatever sum or proportion of the net proceeds of (eventual) sale the court thinks proper. A 'charge' over the property means that when it is sold, the charge (which is like a mortgage) comes into effect and the other spouse will get his or her money out of the proceeds. The husband does not have the right to intervene in respect of the property by virtue of such a charge – his position becomes just like that of a bank or building society to whom money is secured on the property.

In either case, the court specifies at what point the husband can realise his interest in the house. This is likely to be when the youngest child of the family comes of age or when any child undergoing full-time education ceases to remain normally resident in the home. The husband may be given the right to apply to enforce the sale or the charge at any time if the ex-wife marries again or cohabits. If she has to borrow the money to pay off the charge, rather than to buy out her husband's share, she will not get tax relief on the interest on the loan.

### selling later

A difficult problem is whether the house should be kept as a home for the ex-wife even after the children have left home. The court will take into account whether the wife's share of the proceeds if the house were sold then would enable her to buy another house, and also the husband's need for the capital. The court can make only a guesstimate of what the situation is likely to be possibly 12 or 15 years ahead – what money the ex-wife would receive from the sale of the house, her likelihood of employment and earnings and mortgage capacity. Her share would need to be sufficient for her to buy a flat or a smaller house at an age when she is unlikely to be able to raise much by way of mortgage on, probably, low earnings. Meanwhile, the husband will have been able to start afresh with another mortgage because of his lower age and higher earnings at the time of the divorce.

(When the house is eventually sold, liability for capital gains tax may arise for an ex-spouse who is still a joint-owner but who had moved out of the house.)

If it seems likely that the ex-wife will have insufficient to enable her to buy another house then, the court may either award her a larger share or defer the sale (or enforcement of the ex-husband's charge) for the remainder of her life (or until she marries or cohabits) unless by not selling, the ex-husband's problems are likely to outweigh the ex-wife's.

Where either party was legally aided and the legal aid fund's statutory charge applies, this will not be levied until the house is sold. By then, inflation may have reduced the practical effect of the charge.

If she is paying off the mortgage on the house, the wife will be contributing to the value of the husband's eventual share of the proceeds of sale. If, however, there is no mortgage to be paid off, she will effectively be living in the house at the ex-husband's expense. The court therefore may make an order requiring her to pay the ex-husband an occupation rent from the time that the children cease to need the house as a home.

## if mortgaged

Mortgages cannot simply be transferred and the court has no power to order the transfer of a mortgage – only the property subject to the mortgage. The consent of the building society or other mortgagee is necessary, otherwise the mortgagor (usually the husband) remains liable for the mortgage even if the property is transferred. The mortgagees must be served with notice of an application to the court for a transfer of ownership and have the right to object.

The building society or other mortgagee must agree before the transfer can take effect. If they do not agree to the transfer, it may be necessary to pay off the mortgage and find a new mortgagee.

It may well be the ex-wife who is going to be responsible for meeting the mortgage repayments in future, possibly out of an income from maintenance payments on which the building society or bank would not have agreed to make a mortgage loan. It is advisable for a wife to contact the mortgagees as soon as possible and discuss ways of making repayments if and when the house is transferred.

It is not uncommon for building societies to ask a former husband to guarantee a mortgage being taken out by a woman whose income comes from his maintenance payments either in whole or in part. The ex-husband would have to meet the mortgage repayments only if his former wife defaulted. (He can ask her for an indemnity so that she is liable to compensate him if this did happen.) In practice, it is likely to happen only if he defaults on the maintenance.

*where there is an endowment mortgage*
A mortgage on an endowment basis is linked to an insurance policy that will pay out enough to repay the loan (with a surplus if it is a with-profits policy) at the end of the mortgage term or on the policyholder's death.

The application for a property adjustment order where there is an endowment mortgage should include an application to transfer the husband's beneficial interest in the insurance policy to the wife. If this is not transferred and she were to sell the house before the end of the mortgage term, the ex-wife could get nothing from the policy and would have to pay off the whole mortgage loan out of the proceeds of sale. When the mortgage term comes to an end, a decision has to be made regarding any bonuses on the policy over and above the amount required to repay the loan. This surplus could be ordered to go to the husband to compensate for the loss of use of capital, or to the wife who has been paying the premiums for many years, or to be shared between them.

*tax relief on mortgage interest*

On a loan to buy (or improve) your home, tax relief on the whole of the interest is available on up to £30,000 of loan. If the loan exceeds £30,000, interest on the excess is not eligible for tax relief. So, a loan of £40,000 attracts tax relief on only three-quarters of the interest.

Where the loan does not exceed £30,000, the standard rate of tax (27% for 1987/88) is deducted from the monthly interest payable to the building society or other lender. This is known as 'mortgage interest relief at source' (MIRAS).

Tax relief is available to you only if the property is the only or main residence of yourself or of your former (or separated) spouse and provided you still retain an interest in the former home yourself.

If the house remains in joint names, you would get tax relief if you paid the mortgage interest direct – but only up to £30,000 in all in respect of loans on that house and any home of your own.

If you transfer the former home to your spouse outright and go on making the mortgage payments direct, you do not qualify for the tax relief. So, if you wish to contribute to the mortgage payments on the former matrimonial home that has been transferred out of your name, it could make sense to pay the extra to your former spouse in the form of maintenance because on this you will get tax relief.

When your ex-spouse takes over the former matrimonial home and the responsibility for repayment of the mortgage, you will be free to get the full amount of tax relief on any mortgage up to £30,000 taken out by yourself to buy a new home.

**when the house is sold**

Where the court orders the sale of the home and a division of the proceeds, the respective shares can be expressed in percentage terms or fixed figures.

A percentage share may be the better decision. If one party

agreed to accept a fixed sum from the proceeds of sale and the property fetches far more than was anticipated, he or she would lose out and it would be impossible to rectify this because the court has no power to vary a property order once it is made.

A fixed figure may be ordered, however, where the court awards the wife a higher share solely in order that she can buy another home. It is then usually better if the order is for payment of a specific sum, carefully calculated to take account of possible delays in sale. (It is important that the amount of any statutory legal aid charge is also taken into account.) If that were not done and the property sold for less than anticipated, the whole point of the exercise would be defeated.

# the contents of the home

Property adjustment orders can include the contents of the family home. The person who is to remain in the home may apply to have the essential furniture and furnishings of the house transferred to her or him. Any agreement as to contents could be included in the order about the house, to avoid later uncertainty, by annexing an agreed inventory to the order.

You should try to avoid calling on the court to make the allocation for you. A sensible, practical approach is to negotiate with each other who is to have what, and then these assets can be ignored when calculating the capital of each spouse. If, however, the wife accepts that the husband should have, for example, the set of Chippendale chairs, because they belonged to his family, then their value may well be relevant in the eventual adjustment of property.

Where both husband and wife have similar assets, these do not necessarily cancel each other out. For example, where the husband has a company car and the wife has the family car, some adjustments may have to be made for the fact that

○ the husband does not have to pay for maintenance of the company car
○ a lot of his private mileage may be paid for
○ he may have free membership of a motoring organisation
○ his insurance and road tax may be paid for

but he does not have an asset he can sell, whereas the wife's car can be sold.

Remember that items on hire purchase still not paid for cannot be transferred to another's name.

An inventory with estimated values is useful, preferably prepared jointly or by one side for agreement by the other. Whether it is worth getting an expert valuation depends on the amount or value involved, the cost of the valuation, and the degree of dispute. It is rarely worth getting an expert valuation unless the items are of great value, such as antiques.

### disputes
If you cannot agree on anything else, try to agree about the splitting up of the contents – furniture and effects. It will not be worth fighting this out in court unless there are some exceptionally valuable items.

Court proceedings over furniture or household belongings can often be protracted and expensive out of all proportion to the value of the property. They can result in a decision that is not what either party really wanted, and can lead to a forced sale.

### *ownership*
Under section 17 of the Married Women's Property Act 1882, an application can be made to the county court or the High Court by either of the spouses at any time up to 3 years after the decree absolute, even if the applicant has married again, to resolve the question of the ownership of any property (other than the house, if this has been dealt with in the divorce).

Orders made on divorce are, however, often couched in such a way as to resolve such issues finally and prevent subsequent applications under the MWPA.

When determining whether an applicant has an interest at all in the disputed property and, if so, how much, the court will take into account any contribution made by either spouse to its purchase or improvement, in the form of cash or physical work. Proof of where the money came from that was used to buy an item is important. Remember that receipts show only who physically paid the bill, not the source of the money with which it was paid.

When it is necessary to determine the ownership of pieces of furniture, jewellery, antiques or similar belongings under the Married Women's Property Act, the court is likely to decide that

○ any items owned by either of the couple before the marriage remain the property of that person
○ any items subsequently bought by either spouse out of his or her own money are the property of that person
○ any items bought jointly are jointly owned
○ any items bought by the wife out of savings from her housekeeping money are jointly owned
○ any assets bought out of a joint bank account into which both have paid money are jointly owned
○ gifts to one of the couple remain his or her property
○ gifts to both belong normally to the person from whose side of the family the gift came; where the gift was from a common friend, it is usually held to be jointly owned (this applies not only to wedding presents).

Under the Married Women's Property Act, the court can only establish who is the owner of the property. It can then order that the property be handed over to the established owner or that, if jointly owned, it be sold. On divorce, you could keep the particular items held to be yours under MWPA proceedings, but their value would be taken into account in deciding what was a fair and reasonable overall division of property.

If you are in the process of getting divorced, it is usually better to ask the divorce court to consider a particular issue of ownership under the broader umbrella of the general financial application because under the Married Women's Property Act, the court can direct how the proceeds shall be divided only according to strict legal principles: it does not have discretion to take all the circumstances into account as a court has under divorce legislation, nor to make a transfer of property order.

## capital gains tax

Capital gains tax (CGT) is payable at the rate of 30% on gains arising from the 'disposal of assets'.

A specified amount of gains in any one tax year is exempt. This amount changes each year; in the 1987/88 tax year, it is £6,600. Only one exempt amount is allowed per husband and wife (not £6,600 each) while they are married. In the year of separation, each has a full exempt allowance to use against gains arising in the rest of the tax year after the date of the separation. As with income tax, the crucial date is that of separation not of divorce.

So long as a husband and wife are living together, and for the rest of the tax year after separation, no gain results where there is a disposal between them. But when the asset is eventually transferred to someone else, the gain (or loss) is calculated over the entire period of ownership by both parties.

Inflation is taken into account in assessing gains by reference to increases in the retail prices index (RPI) based on the figure at March 1982.

On divorce or separation, the major areas where disposals are likely to arise are

o household contents
o other assets such as car, a second home, stocks and shares, savings ('assets' means practically everything capable of being owned and sold or transferred)
o the home.

*household contents*
Most consumer goods decrease in value, so the question of 'gain' does not arise. Most chattels with a lifespan of less than fifty years are exempt from CGT, anyway.

*other assets*
Cash and cars are specifically exempt from CGT, and so are any sums received on the surrender of life insurance policies. So if, for one reason or another, you cash in an endowment policy which is linked to a mortgage, there is no question of liability to CGT. A sale of other assets, such as stocks and shares, gives rise to CGT. So, too, does a transfer between spouses after the end of the tax year in which they separated.

## the home

Any gain made on the sale of a person's principal private residence (PPR) is normally exempt from CGT. But CGT liability does arise when the home is sold if you had stopped living there more than two years ago.

On divorce, it is likely that you will do one or other of three things with the home:

○ sell it and split the proceeds
○ transfer it to your spouse outright
○ put it into joint names (or leave it in joint names) and postpone sale and division of the proceeds until a future date.

### sale and division of proceeds
If you sell the house and split the proceeds within two years of one or other of you ceasing to reside there, you will be entitled to claim 'principal private residence' exemption provided the home was your only, or main, residence throughout the period that you owned it.

If at any time you have two or more homes, both are potentially eligible for the exemption. If, therefore, you have bought another home and the old home has not been sold, you may make a choice within two years as to which one you wish to have treated as your principal private residence. If you do not, your tax inspector will. It may make sense to claim the exemption in respect of the house that is being sold, if this is at a gain.

Where the sale takes place more than two years after one of you has left, the person who ceased to reside there will not be fully exempt. Only a portion of the gain will be exempt: namely, the period of his or her actual occupation plus the last two years of ownership. (The last two years of ownership are always exempt.) Thus, the longer you wait beyond two years after separation before selling your old home, the greater the possibility of CGT being payable by the person who left. The person who remains will not be liable to CGT provided he or she has remained permanently in residence.

You will be liable to CGT on a gain if you left the home more than two years ago and, on selling it, you make a profit considerably greater than the increase in the retail prices index since March 1982 or, if you bought it later, since the date of acquisition.

*example*

Herbert and Wilma had bought their home for £7,000 in 1970. They separated in 1975 but only came to sell the house in May 1986 when it was sold for £36,500.

The house was in joint names. Herbert had left when they separated and Wilma remained there. She had no CGT liability because she could claim PPR exemption on her share for the whole period.

Calculation of Herbert's CGT liability was in two stages.

*i) his net gain*

This was half of the difference between the cost of acquisition and the proceeds of sale, with an allowance for inflation between March 1982 and May 1986. The RPI on those dates was 313.4 and 386 respectively, an increase of 72.6 points.

(The value of the retail prices index is published monthly by the Department of Employment and the figures to be used in calculating the indexation allowance for the month of the sale of a house are issued by the Inland Revenue press office, Somerset House, London WC2R 1LB.)

The allowance is arrived at by adding to the cost of acquisition (the price he paid when he bought it) a sum calculated as follows:

$$\text{cost of acquisition} \times \frac{\text{increase in RPI March 82 to May 1986}}{\text{RPI March 82}}$$

$$\text{i.e. for Herbert } £7,000 \times \frac{72.6}{313.4} = £1,621.57$$

Herbert's net gain for capital gains tax purposes is therefore

$$\frac{£36,500 - £8,621}{2} = £13,939$$

*ii) his exemption*

The formula to work out the amount that is exempt under the principal private residence exemption is

$$\text{gain} \times \frac{\text{years of occupation + last 2 years of ownership}}{\text{period of ownership}}$$

$$\text{i.e. for Herbert } £13,939 \times \frac{5+2}{16} = £6,098$$

This reduced Herbert's gain to £7,841 of which £6,300 (the exemption for the tax year 1986/87) was exempt under the annual exemption rule. This left a taxable gain of £1,541.

Herbert's CGT liability on £1,541 at 30% was £462.

Capital gains tax would have been more of an expense if the house had been in Herbert's sole name. The whole of the net gain (£27,878) would then have been his, and the taxable gain would have been £12,196 *minus* £6,300 exemption, giving a tax liability of £1,768. (In such a case, an accountant or solicitor might have advised him to argue that Wilma had acquired an interest in the home during the intervening period because she had, for example, been paying the mortgage.)

### transfer of the home to your spouse outright

Although no money changes hands, the transfer would in theory be a 'disposal', based on the market value at the date of disposal. Quite apart from the fact that there may well not be a capital gain anyway (after taking inflation into account and the current year's exemption), the transaction would qualify for PPR exemption if made within two years of the transferor leaving the house.

Even if the transfer were made outside the two-year period, provided that it was made as part of a divorce settlement and provided that you had not elected to declare any other home as your principal private residence, the Inland Revenue would treat the disposal as exempt by 'concession'.

The date of election is critical, but provided you get the sequence right, liability to CGT will not arise.

### house in joint names sold much later

Transferring the house into joint names will not attract CGT liability.

When the house is sold many years later and the proceeds divided, the spouse who has remained in the home will not have to pay tax on his or her share because that will be fully covered by the PPR exemption. But the one who moved out will be liable to some CGT. In such a case, to save CGT, it could be worth transferring the house fully to the ex-spouse who is living there, subject to a charge to the other ex-spouse. It very much depends on which would give him the biggest potential tax saving. If the house were transferred to the wife subject to a charge in favour of the husband for, say, one third of the net proceeds of sale, the transfer escapes CGT. On realisation of the charge, the husband will be liable for capital gains tax on the increase in the value of the charge after taking into account the increase in the RPI and his annual exemption.

**second home**
Selling a second home to raise money may render you liable to capital gains tax if there is a sufficient gain. (By 'second home' in this context is meant a property for which PPR did not apply while you were living together.)

Transferring it to the spouse who is moving out of the matrimonial home could make more sense. If he or she proposes to live in it as his or her principal private residence, when it is eventually sold it will be possible for him or her to claim PPR exemption on the whole of any gain from the date when the property had first been acquired – provided that the transfer between the spouses takes place before the end of the tax year in which they separate. After that, the transferor will have a CGT liability by reference to the market value of the property at the time of the transfer.

**advice**
You may well feel that you need specialist advice about capital gains tax, perhaps from an accountant. For someone in receipt of legal aid, it might be better for the solicitor to instruct the accountant since he will then pay the accountant's fee and may be able to recover the fee from the legal aid fund as an expense reasonably incurred, but would need to obtain the authority of the Law Society before instructing the accountant. If the accountant were instructed directly, the client would have to find the money more or less straightaway (whereas a legal aid statutory charge may not be payable until considerably later, if at all).

# SCOTLAND
# AND NORTHERN IRELAND

This book deals only with the situation in England and Wales. Here are some very brief indications about Northern Ireland and Scotland.

## Northern Ireland

The law and procedure in matrimonial proceedings in Northern Ireland are, generally speaking, similar to those in England and Wales, except that the Matrimonial and Family Proceedings Act 1984 does not apply in Northern Ireland.

The main differences are that

○ a divorce petition cannot be filed until 3 years after the marriage
○ there are no 'postal' or 'special procedure' divorces in Northern Ireland: the parties must attend the court in person and give their evidence to the judge
○ undefended divorces are available in Northern Ireland in both the High Court and county court at the choice of the petitioner
○ legal aid is available in Northern Ireland for all the divorce proceedings
○ the Matrimonial Homes Act does not apply to Northern Ireland.

## Scotland

The ground for divorce is basically the same in Scotland as England, but the procedure and terminology are quite different, and important new provisions relating to financial arrangements on divorce were introduced in September 1986 under the Family Law (Scotland) Act 1985.

Scottish court procedure can be used only if the Scottish courts have jurisdiction. Divorces may be raised in any sheriff court or in the Court of Session in Edinburgh. (There are no magistrates' courts in Scotland.)

The person seeking the divorce is called 'the pursuer' and the other spouse 'the defender'.

There is no minimum period of marriage before a divorce can be applied for. Decree of divorce when granted is equivalent to the 'decree absolute' – there is no such thing in Scotland as 'decree nisi', although a decree can be appealed against within 21 days of having been granted (14 days in the sheriff court).

### quickie divorces
Where a couple wishes to proceed with a two year consent divorce or a five year divorce, and there are no children of the marriage, or none under 16 years of age, and neither party is making any financial claims, they can proceed by the 'quickie procedure'. The necessary printed forms can be obtained from the court and from citizens advice bureaux.

In two year consent divorces, the pursuer fills in part 1 of the form and sends it to the other spouse who completes part 2 indicating his or her consent. On receipt of that, the pursuer completes the affidavit in part 3, swearing the affidavit before a notary public (most solicitors are notaries public) or a justice of the peace, then forwards to the court the completed forms with the extract marriage certificate (photocopies are not acceptable) and a remittance for the court dues. The court takes all the administrative steps (such as service of documents) from then on and advises the parties when decree of divorce is granted. No appearance of the parties in court is necessary.

In five year separation divorces, the procedure is similar but consent is not necessary and part 2 is in the form of an affidavit which is sworn before a notary public or justice of the peace.

The court dues are at present £40. Any pursuer who is in receipt of supplementary benefit or of family income supplement or who is getting advice and assistance under the legal aid scheme does not need to pay the court dues.

**non-quickie divorces**
Where there are children of the marriage under 16 years of age and/or the pursuer is making financial claims, it is necessary to go through a more complicated procedure and you should get the advice of a solicitor.

Legal advice and assistance is available, under the equivalent of the 'green form' scheme in England, for preliminary advice and assistance with obtaining the necessary evidence. A grant of civil legal aid can be applied for in connection with the court proceedings. The financial eligibility limits and application procedures are much the same as in England but the scheme is administered by the Scottish Legal Aid Board rather than the Law Society of Scotland.

A summons or initial writ is lodged in court and served on the other party by the pursuer's solicitor. If the case is to be defended, the opponent (defender) has to intimate to the court that he or she is defending the case, and thereafter has to lodge defences, and the case proceeds to hearing.

If the action is not defended, the divorce proceeds by way of 'affidavit procedure'. The pursuer and a supporting or corroborating witness have to swear affidavits which are lodged in court. If the judge is satisfied with the evidence, decree of divorce will be granted.

The pursuer's affidavit also has to deal with arrangements for any children of the marriage under 16 years of age and to narrate as far as is known the financial position of both parties. Where there are children involved, an affidavit has to be lodged and sworn by a person who is not a party to the action, speaking to the accommodation available for the children, and speaking generally to the welfare of the children. This affidavit can be sworn by a person who is a near relative, perhaps the grandmother or grandfather of the children.

In an undefended action, even where there are children involved, it is not necessary for the pursuer to appear in court or before a judge in chambers. If the judge is satisfied with the affidavits, including the evidence about the arrangements for the welfare of the children, decree of divorce will be pronounced.

## occupying the home
It is important to seek legal advice as to the extent of any rights of occupancy you might have under the Matrimonial Homes (Family Protection) (Scotland) Act 1981, because once you are no longer married, these rights cease. For example

o the spouse who is not tenant of the matrimonial home (and the other spouse is) has occupancy rights and cannot be excluded from the home
o the spouse who is not the joint owner of the matrimonial home has occupancy rights and cannot be excluded.

But the court granting divorce can make orders about the occupation of the home and the use of its contents. There are provisions for transfer of tenancy, exclusion of violent spouses, and other aspects regulating rights in the matrimonial home. For example, a joint owner can be prevented from forcing a sale of the matrimonial home.

## financial claims
The court has to apply specific principles in deciding on orders for financial provision and the division of matrimonial property. 'Matrimonial property' basically means the property accumulated during the marriage but excluding, for example, inheritance received by either spouse during the marriage; specifically included under the new Act are rights under pension policies. The court is empowered to make detailed orders, for example, for capital payments by instalments and orders for the transfer of matrimonial property, such as the

home. Matrimonial property is to be shared equally unless there are special circumstances that justify other proportions.

*lump sum and property transfer*
Once decree of divorce has been granted, it is not possible to apply to the court for a capital sum payment or for a transfer of property order. It is very important, therefore, to seek legal advice when raising divorce proceedings to find out whether you should apply for such an order.

The court must see whether a claim for financial provision can be met by a lump sum or a transfer of property before awarding a periodical allowance.

*maintenance*
A maintenance award (called 'periodical allowance') for a wife or husband is part of the obligation of aliment owed by one spouse to the other (and by a parent to his or her child).

The pursuer can apply to the court in the divorce proceedings for an order for periodical allowance. The defender also can apply for maintenance, although it is less likely that a husband will be granted an award of maintenance by the court.

Under the 1985 Act, periodical allowance is to be awarded only for a period of 3 years after divorce, to allow the ex-spouse to adjust to the loss of financial support. Where, however, there are young children and it is not practicable for the wife to obtain employment or where, for instance, the wife is of an age where it is virtually impossible for her to obtain employment, the 3-year 'rule' may not be applied. It is likely that the onus will be on the wife to show why the 3-year limit should not apply.

*variation*
After decree of divorce has been pronounced, application can be made to vary the periodical allowance awarded or to obtain a maintenance award where there was no award in the original proceedings, but this depends on the applicant satisfying the

court that there has been a material change in circumstances. The variation may be upwards or downwards. Any right of an ex-spouse to maintenance ceases on his or her death or remarriage.

The new 3-year rule for maintenance awards will limit the time span for applying for a variation.

### for children

Claims for maintenance for children should be made in the divorce proceedings by the person having custody of the children. For example, where it is agreed which spouse shall have custody, that spouse can defend the proceedings to get a formal award of custody from the court and to obtain aliment (that is, maintenance) for the children.

Application can be made both for non-residential and residential (staying) access by any party showing an interest.

### tax consequences

Tax relief is granted on maintenance payments under a court order. It is important to seek advice to make sure maintenance orders are arranged in such a way as to obtain the most advantageous tax benefits. The tax arrangements in respect of small maintenance payments apply also in Scotland.

Where an order for maintenance payments for children to be made to the custodial parent in trust for each child (so that the parent is obliged to spend the money on the child rather than on him/herself) states that the aliment is the child's and is being paid to the parent as the child's guardian, the parent is not assessed for tax on the payments which count as the child's income and eligible for each child's personal tax allowance.

Payments to a child under an agreement "registered for execution" are tax effective.

The Scottish Association of Citizens Advice Bureaux has published *Splitting up*, by David Nichols, a guide to separation and divorce in Scotland (£2 from CABx).

# COSTS

A solicitor charges a privately paying client the full amount of all costs incurred. The charges made in his bill will be based on the hours spent by the solicitor preparing the case at his own charge-out rate, with a mark-up for what solicitors call 'care and attention'. The basic hourly rate (anything from £25 to £100) depends on the firm of solicitors and the area of the country; the mark-up (anything from 25% to 60%, or more), on the importance of the subject matter.

You are entitled to query your solicitor's bill and to ask for a fully itemised account, with details of time spent and disbursements. If still dissatisfied, you are entitled to have the bill 'taxed'.

A solicitor is not entitled to sue for his or her bill on a contentious matter unless he gives a month's notice to the client with a reminder of the client's right to have the bill taxed.

### taxation of costs

Taxation is the process whereby the registrar at the county court considers the bill and decides whether the charges made are fair and reasonable in the circumstances of the particular case.

For taxation, the bill has to be drawn up in a specially detailed form, in chronological order of the steps taken. The solicitor can charge also for attendance at court to determine the figure to be paid.

There is a court fee for the taxation of costs: so many pence (currently 5p) per £ of the final taxed costs.

## costs awarded

If you want your spouse to pay at least a part of your legal costs, a request 'for costs' should be made at each stage of the proceedings, whenever orders are sought. Don't forget this.

In divorce matters, there is not just one set of proceedings: apart from the obtaining of the decree, there may be matters of litigation on maintenance, property adjustment, custody, access – all of which run up costs. At the conclusion of each such hearing, you can ask the registrar or judge for an order for costs and he decides there and then whether to make such an order.

If you are asking the court to make an order by consent (that is, in terms agreed with your spouse), one of the agreed terms can be in respect of costs.

Costs may be awarded by the court on a party-and-party basis or on a solicitor-and-own-client basis or (the highest level) on a common fund basis.

The amount payable when there is an order for costs (which means party-and-party costs unless otherwise specified) is usually about 60% to 80% of the actual bill charged by the solicitor to his or her client. So, even if you secure an order for costs, you will not have your bill met in full. It is only in exceptional circumstances that your spouse will be ordered to pay a higher rate of costs – namely, either common fund or solicitor-and-own-client. If you are legally aided, costs are generally awarded on a common fund basis and should meet your potential legal aid liability in full; if you are paying privately, a solicitor-and-own-client order should have this effect.

When an order for costs is made and a figure cannot be agreed, the bill is taxed, on a party-and-party basis. This should be done within 3 months of the date of the order for costs.

It is very rare to obtain an order for more than costs on a party-and-party basis, and the court will bear in mind, at a final financial hearing, the effect of any order for costs and will be conscious, for example, that such an order would still leave the recipient with a part of the overall bill to meet. Sometimes, the amount of the wife's share in any property is increased to take account of her liability for her own costs rather than an order for costs made against the husband.

If someone on legal aid is ordered to pay the other party's costs, the legal aid certificate does not cover this: the person has to pay out of his or her own pocket. The court must determine the amount that is reasonable for the legally aided person to pay. It may limit the amount of such costs to the equivalent of the person's legal aid contributions and make the costs payable over 12 months.

There are proposals to change to what will be called a 'standard' basis, covering the present party-and-party costs and including common fund costs under a legal aid certificate, and an 'indemnity' basis, covering the present solicitor-and-own-client costs, with some differences in the amounts recoverable. The effect of the proposed changes is likely to be that an order for costs will amount to a rather greater proportion than at present.

● for the divorce

The petitioner can ask for costs (although this is not usual where the petition is on the basis of two years' separation with consent). If an order for costs is made, the petitioner's solicitor has his or her charges assessed by reference to the scale laid down by the Matrimonial Causes (Costs) Rules.

*example*

The wife goes to see a solicitor to obtain a simple divorce based on her husband's adultery. She has to settle up with her own solicitor. She obtains an order for costs, assessed on the fixed scale at £125. But she had insisted on 'five star' service, requiring the solicitor to come personally to her house, spending many hours discussing the matter, and speaking to him many times on the telephone to find out how the case was progressing, and her solicitor's bill came to £400. She has to pay the £275 difference herself.

A similar situation could arise where the wife, instead of consulting local solicitors, had instructed expensive upmarket solicitors to conduct the divorce for her: again, this is a luxury for which she herself must pay.

● for an injunction

Injunction proceedings can run up very substantial costs. The successful applicant should obtain an order for costs against the respondent. But in many cases, this may not be worth the paper it is written on, either because the respondent disappears or because he is a 'man of straw' – without any funds.

● custody and access

Considerable costs can be run up in disputes over custody and access. The fact that one parent obtains custody rather than the other does not necessarily mean that that parent has 'won' in the same sense as would be the case in, for example, a claim for damages for personal injuries. So, both parties may be left to bear their own costs. The court is only likely to order one party to pay the other's costs if that one's behaviour during the proceedings has been in some way quite unreasonable, causing unnecessary delays and expense.

● financial matters

The fact that the wife obtains an order for maintenance or an order relating to the matrimonial home does not necessarily mean that she will be awarded costs – but the impact of costs is likely to be taken into account in making the overall order.

Sometimes a husband's solicitors will at an early stage offer to pay the wife's costs in order to try to force a settlement.

**example of how costs may be awarded**

H and W, both in their late twenties, had been married 3½ years. There were no children. W has obtained a divorce based on H's adultery. They both have successful careers so there is no question of maintenance, and neither of them is eligible for legal aid. The former matrimonial home, in which H is still living, was bought by him before the marriage with a mortgage of £10,000, the balance being paid from his own savings and from a legacy. The house is now worth £40,000 after deduction of the outstanding mortgage. Neither party has any other significant capital.

W brings proceedings for financial provision, claiming a lump sum of £15,000. H fights this on the basis that because of the length of the marriage and the fact that the purchase of the house was entirely financed by him, and that W has sufficient earnings to obtain a mortgage herself, she should receive, if anything, only a small lump sum. The matter proceeds to a hearing, at which the registrar makes an order in W's favour for a lump sum of £7,500. By now, they have run up legal fees of £1,500 (£750 each).

The alternatives in these circumstances are:

(i) W gets an order for **party-and-party costs**

|  | £ |  | £ |
|---|---|---|---|
| W gets |  | cost to H |  |
| lump sum from H | 7,500 | lump sum to W | 7,500 |
| *less*: own legal fees | 750 | own legal fees | 750 |
|  |  | costs payable to W | 600 |
|  | 6,750 |  | 8,850 |
| *add* costs paid by H | 600 |  |  |
| W gets | 7,350 |  |  |

(ii) W gets order for **half costs**

It is possible that because W has run up unnecessary costs in fighting the action, the registrar feels that she is not entitled to all her party-and-party costs, and makes an order for half the costs to be paid by H. The effect of this in the above example is that W would end up getting £7,050 with the cost to H being £8,550.

## (iii)  H's solicitor makes a **'Calderbank' offer**

To protect H from having to pay two lots of costs as well as a lump sum, his solicitor wrote at an early stage a 'without prejudice' letter, making an offer of a settlement of £9,000 in all and to pay her costs on a party-and-party basis. Because the offer was 'without prejudice' it was privileged and could not be revealed to the registrar without the consent of both parties.

The letter, however, went on to say that the offeror reserved the right to bring the letter to the court's attention on the question of costs at the conclusion of the case if W is awarded less than the £9,000 (a 'Calderbank letter'. Under the principles of the case of Calderbank v Calderbank, if she is awarded less than the amount H offered, she will have to pay his party-and-party costs from the date of the offer up to the hearing and he will be ordered to pay her party-and-party costs only up to the date of the offer.) W did not accept and went ahead with her claim for £15,000.

At the stage when H wrote the letter offering £9,000 in settlement, the parties' costs were only £250 each. If W had accepted, the position would have been

|  | £ |  | £ |
|---|---|---|---|
| W would have got |  | cost to H |  |
| lump sum from H | 9,000 | lump sum to W | 9,000 |
| *less*: own costs | 250 | own costs | 250 |
|  | 8,750 | costs payable to W | 200 |
| costs payable by H | 200 |  | 9,450 |
|  | 8,950 |  |  |

Since W refused and pressed on with the claim (getting an order for a lump sum of £7,500) and costs on both sides have run up to £750 each, the position is now as follows:

| | £ | | £ |
|---|---|---|---|
| W gets | | cost to H | |
| lump sum from H | 7,500 | lump sum to W | 7,500 |
| *less*: own legal costs | 750 | own costs | 750 |
| H's costs | | W's costs payable to | |
| payable since offer | 400 | date of offer | 200 |
| | 6,350 | | 8,450 |
| *add* own costs before | | *less*: own costs | |
| date of offer, | | after offer, | |
| payable by H | 200 | payable by W | 400 |
| | 6,550 | | 8,050 |

H has substantially improved his position on costs by making a realistic offer at an early stage. W, by not accepting the 'Calderbank' offer, has gambled away £2,400 – the difference between what she would have got if she had settled and what she eventually got in pursuit of another £6,000 (the difference between what she was offered in settlement and what she was originally claiming). H, as it happens, pitched his offer about right, and saved himself £1,400 in the process.

In this example, the parties were at least fighting over an asset of some substance, but supposing that instead of the house being worth £40,000, it had been worth only £20,000, and the wife's initial claim was for £7,000, it is unlikely that the costs on both sides would have been significantly lower, so that the percentage impact of the costs consequences of a 'Calderbank' offer would be even greater.

A 'Calderbank' offer is a lottery unless you or your solicitor can accurately forecast what order the court is likely to award and unless the build-up of the costs has been properly monitored. It is part of the job of an experienced divorce lawyer to keep in touch with the level of awards being made by the courts and especially with the kind of awards usually made by the local registrars.

A rejected 'Calderbank' offer should be reviewed from time to time: by the one who turned it down in case the terms have become reasonable with the passing of time, and by the offeror who may now wish to increase an offer made some time ago.

**when costs are paid**
The theoretical (and usually the practical) position is that the
successful party has to pay his or her own solicitor's bill first
and then recover any contribution ordered by the court from
the other party. Usually, the solicitor will continue to act by
preparing the bill and having it taxed and enforced against the
payer.

Sometimes the solicitor may not press his client for payment
of that part of his costs which are recoverable from the paying
party but that is entirely a matter of the solicitor's benevolence
and his assessment of the prospect of the other side paying up.

# CHANGE IN CIRCUMSTANCES

A lump sum or property adjustment order, once made, cannot be varied nor can you go back to court to obtain another one, nor ask for one later if not included in the original application. Although a lump sum order cannot be varied, if the lump sum is being paid in instalments, the size and frequency of instalments can be varied, but not so as to alter the total of the lump sum originally awarded.

With a periodical payments order, even if a spouse had merely a nominal order of, say, 5p per year, which has not expired because of either remarriage or an originally imposed time limit, it is possible to apply to the court to have the order varied – that is, for the amount payable to be increased or decreased, or even for the order to be brought to an end – if it can be shown that there has been a material change in the financial circumstances of either party. You can apply on your own behalf and/or on behalf of your children.

An application for a variation can be made at any time on or after the decree nisi, even many years later provided that the recipient has not married again. There is no limit on the number of variations that can be applied for.

The court can also vary any agreement that the couple had made between themselves, even though they may have agreed not to refer the agreement to the court. In law, any term in an agreement that precludes one party from seeking the assistance of the courts is void.

An order which was expressed to be final as to both capital and income cannot be varied, and a separation agreement so expressed is likely to be upheld.

If an application for maintenance made previously was

formally dismissed by the court, the application cannot be revived later.

## applying for a variation

An application can be made at the divorce court where the order you want to vary was made. If that original court is now inconvenient, you can ask for the case to be transferred to one more convenient for you. (If the order was registered in a magistrates' court, that is the court to which you must apply: you cannot apply to the court which originally made the order.)

The application should be made on the standard form of notice of application, available from the court office. You may wish to lodge the application as soon as possible so that any variation of periodical payments can be backdated to the date of the application. You do not have to accompany the application with an affidavit but you may need to file an affidavit in order to spur your ex-spouse into responding to the application. He or she then has to file an affidavit in reply, within 14 days. Your affidavit should give up-to-date details of your financial position and why you feel a variation is (or is not) appropriate. The court fee is £15 (no fee if consent order).

### reasons for an application
Major factors that are likely to affect financial orders made in the divorce court are

○ a change in financial circumstances of the payer or payee, including retirement
○ remarriage of the payee (periodical payments order ends)
○ cohabitation of the payee
○ remarriage or cohabitation of the payer
○ death of either
○ either becoming disabled
○ children getting older (or the father getting richer).

If the court rejects the application for a variation, this does not preclude an application for a variation being made at some later stage if circumstances change again.

## the court's approach

The court must consider all the circumstances of the case anew, as well as any change in circumstances, giving first consideration to the welfare of any child of the family under 18. The court must also consider whether in all the circumstances it would now be appropriate to vary an order for periodical payments so that the payments are only for such further period as would be sufficient to enable the recipient to adjust without undue hardship to the termination of the payments, or to terminate the payments altogether – 'a clean break'.

On an application for a variation, the court does not have power to order a clean break arrangement consisting of an immediate capital payment with discharge of any maintenance order. But in a recent (1986) case, the court decided that it could allow the paying party to give an undertaking to pay a capital sum and that it would be fair for the recipient's periodical payments to cease once the capital sum was paid.

## marriage of ex-spouse

On remarriage, a former wife's right to maintenance ceases immediately and cannot be revived against that ex-husband even if she finds herself on her own again – divorced, separated or widowed.

There is no formal requirement to tell the previous husband that she has married again, but if she does not do so and he finds out, he can ask her to repay what he has paid her since her new marriage; if she does not pay up, he can sue her for the overpaid money as a debt.

Maintenance payments to or for children are not automatically affected by the mother's new marriage, but the remarriage of either parent may give rise to a situation in which a variation is justified.

An ex-wife's right to occupy what had been the matrimonial home may cease on remarriage. The terms of the court order may require the house now to be sold and the proceeds divided in the specified proportions.

If you made a lump sum payment of, say, £20,000 to your ex-spouse and six months later you hear that she or he has remarried, you cannot apply for a variation. (In rare cases, an application to have the order set aside on the grounds of fraud, or non-disclosure of the intention to remarry, may succeed.) Where a lump sum has been ordered to be paid in instalments and the recipient ex-spouse marries again, instalments have to be continued until the full amount is paid.

### cohabitation

If you are paying your ex-spouse maintenance and she cohabits with another man, you may have grounds to apply to the court for a variation of the order. The court will normally expect it to be proved that there is some permanence to the cohabitation and that it is reasonable to infer that there is financial contribution from the cohabitant.

If you are paying maintenance to your ex-spouse and children and you set up home with someone who already has children, which involves you in additional expenses, this does not mean that your obligations to your former spouse and children cease. If you apply for a variation, the court will take into account your new obligations even though you are not married, but these will normally be expected to take second place to your obligations to the children of your previous marriage.

### retirement

In the case of either the recipient's or the payer's retirement, an application should be made to vary the order by the party who is feeling the pinch. In these circumstances, the one-third formula is generally less relevant than the 'net effect' formula. Usually, the court is concerned to try to share out the more limited finances fairly.

## variation of a magistrates' court order

Magistrates' court orders also can be varied, either upward or downward, where there has been a change in circumstances.

If the couple subsequently divorce, this will not necessarily bring a magistrates' court order to an end. An order made during the marriage will end automatically only if the divorce court substitutes its own order. If not, the magistrates' court order will continue, and also the right to apply for a variation. The order will cease automatically on the recipient's remarriage or death. If the payer remarries, this does not affect the order but may provide grounds for variation.

In the case of a lump sum, the position is different to that in divorce proceedings: there is apparently no restriction on when and how often a lump sum may be applied for (subject to the £500 limit each time).

### registered order

If a divorce court order has been registered in the magistrates' court, application for a variation has to be made to the magistrates' court. The magistrates' court cannot discharge a divorce court order but can vary the amount of the order on application. No affidavits are required and the magistrates will not have before them the information and calculations (for instance, about tax) on which the registrar at the divorce court based his original order. So, unless they are provided with full up-to-date information about the parties' finances, they may reduce the order unrealistically.

### when on supplementary benefit

Maintenance paid by a husband counts in full as income for supplementary benefit calculations. Unless the maintenance that the husband could pay is more than the total supplementary benefit payable, there is little point in a woman seeking an increase in her maintenance because she will still only be topped up to the same 'needs' level by the DHSS; if maintenance increases, therefore, supplementary benefit decreases. Occasional presents to an ex-wife or children are not counted as income so it would be better to concentrate on getting these, where possible.

Registration of a maintenance order in the magistrates' court is useful when the amount of maintenance is equal to or less than the rate of any supplementary benefit the recipient would be entitled to. When the order is registered, the payments due under the order can be assigned by the woman to the DHSS who will then pay her the full amount of her supplementary benefit entitlement, irrespective of whether any payments are made by the man or not. This saves anxiety and inconvenience if he does not pay up.

Where the amount of the order is greater than the supplementary benefit entitlement, payments by the DHSS will be limited to the amount of supplementary benefit the woman is entitled to.

The DHSS have a duty to the public to try to recover the money they pay out to someone on supplementary benefit from the person responsible for supporting the claimant. Thus, if a court order has been made, they will seek its enforcement and regular variation upwards. If no order exists, they will ask the man for voluntary payments; should he refuse, they will ask the woman to go to court for an order.

The DHSS can ask the woman if she agrees to take a case in the magistrates' court against the man to try and make him pay (called 'liable relative' proceedings). If she does not want to do this (for instance, because she wants to encourage cooperation with her ex-husband in other areas), the DHSS should not try to persuade her, but can take proceedings themselves to enforce the order that has been assigned to them. A man is not legally responsible for supporting and maintaining his ex-wife unless ordered by a court to pay maintenance to her. If he refuses to pay the due amount and the DHSS are satisfied that he has the means to pay, they can take him to court under 'liable relative' proceedings.

## death of former spouse

When the recipient dies, the payer can immediately stop any maintenance payments. But any outstanding instalments of a lump sum become due to the deceased's estate, and an unfulfilled transfer of property order can be enforced by the estate.

If the person paying maintenance dies, the maintenance order comes to an end (unless the order was for secured payments). The former spouse may be able to apply to the court under the Inheritance (Provision for Family and Dependants) Act 1975 for financial provision out of the deceased's estate (unless the court has previously ordered that such a claim shall not be made). An application can also be made by or on behalf of a child. The application must be made within six months of probate being granted – to be safe, make sure the application is lodged as soon as possible.

Death of the payer in Scotland does not terminate periodical allowance but executors can apply for the payment to be reduced, recalled or commuted. (The 1975 Inheritance Act does not apply in Scotland.)

### *other help on death*

Occupational pension schemes normally provide a lump sum death benefit (of up to four times the member's pay) when the member of the scheme dies before retirement. After the divorce, it is likely that the ex-husband will have changed the name of the person he wishes to receive the money on his death, so that his ex-wife may not benefit. The decision whether to pay any sum to her would, however, ultimately rest with the trustees of the pension scheme.

### life insurance

Because maintenance payments will cease when the payer dies, it may be advisable on divorce for the spouse who is going to be dependent on payments from the other to take out a life insurance policy on the payer's life. And the parent who does not have care and control of the children may want to take out an insurance policy on the life of the parent who is looking after the children, so that if that parent were to die while the children are still dependent, some money would become available towards the extra cost to the other parent of then taking on responsibility for the children.

The policy could be a whole-life policy whereby the sum assured is paid out whenever it may be that the person dies or a 'term' insurance which pays out a set sum on death within so many years, taken out for the period of likely dependence. Premiums for term policies are generally lower than for other types of life insurance. There are some term insurance policies, called 'family income benefit' policies, where instead of one lump sum on the insured person's death, regular sums are paid (say, every quarter) for the balance of the insured period.

### a will

A will made by either husband or wife is not automatically revoked on divorce, but the will is interpreted as if the ex-spouse had died on the day before the divorce: any gift left to him or her goes to whoever is entitled to the residue of the estate. Where the terms of the will give the residue to the former spouse, this will be dealt with in accordance with the intestacy rules. If the ex-spouse is named as executor, that appointment will be of no effect.

If there is no will and a divorced person's estate has to be dealt with under the intestacy rules, the former spouse will not be taken into account in the distribution of the estate. But any children remain eligible for their share of an inheritance.

In Northern Ireland, a will is not affected by divorce. In Scotland, bequests to husband/wife are not automatically invalidated by subsequent divorce.

It is advisable to make a (new) will when divorce proceedings are started, in case you die before the decree absolute. But remember that if you marry again, marriage automatically revokes an earlier will (except in Scotland) unless it was made in contemplation of that marriage.

## national insurance after a divorce

Divorce does not affect a man's national insurance contribution position. Nor does it affect that of a woman who is paying self-employed (class 2 and class 4) contributions or the standard rate of employed (class 1) contributions at the time. After divorce, each continues to pay as before.

It is not so straightforward for any other woman. An employed woman who, before the divorce, had been paying class 1 contributions at the married woman's reduced rate, is treated as a single person from the date on which the decree is made absolute and therefore becomes liable to pay the full class 1 rate. She should tell her employer and get from him her 'certificate of reduced liability' or 'certificate of election' to send back to her local DHSS office. The full class 1 contributions will be deducted from her wages from then on.

Any employee whose earnings are below a specified minimum (£39 a week for the 1987/88 tax year), or anyone who is not earning at all, does not have to pay national insurance contributions, but can pay class 3 contributions voluntarily; these give a woman, for example, the right to claim maternity grant and retirement pension. DHSS leaflet NI 42 gives information about making voluntary contributions.

A woman over the age of 60 does not have to pay national insurance contributions.

There are various free DHSS leaflets explaining the position about contributions and benefits in specific circumstances: leaflet NI 95 is a guide for divorced women. If you are at all unsure of your position, get advice from your local social security office in writing (and keep it safe) or a citizens advice bureau may be able to help to clear up any queries. Detailed information about contributory benefits under the national insurance scheme is given in the Child Poverty Action Group's *Guide to non-means-tested social security benefits* (1987 edition £4.50 from CPAG, 1-5 Bath Street, London EC1V 9PY).

*woman's retirement pension*

The payment of the state retirement pension to a divorced
woman depends on her age when she got divorced and on
whether it is based on her own or her former husband's
national insurance record (or a combination of both).

A woman divorced under the age of 60 can have her former
husband's contributions added to her own record if that helps
her qualify for a retirement pension when the time comes, or
gains her a larger pension. If, however, she marries again
before she is 60, she can no longer make use of her previous
husband's record: she has to rely on her new husband's record
or on contributions she has made herself.

If a woman who is approaching 60 can time the decree
absolute to follow closely on her attaining the age of 60, she
may qualify for retirement pension immediately, without having to have contributed at all herself. If, however, the decree is
made absolute before her 60th birthday, she may have to pay
contributions for the intervening period in order to be eligible
for a full pension.

A woman already aged 60 may qualify for a retirement
pension immediately the divorce is made absolute, even if her
former husband has not yet retired. The amount of pension
she gets depends on his contribution record: it is the amount
she would have received had he died on the date of the decree
absolute.

If a divorced woman marries again after the age of 60, any
pension based on her previous husband's national insurance
contributions continues to be paid, despite her second marriage. But if her new husband's record would give her a higher
pension, that may be used instead.

The basis for earning a state retirement pension changed in
April 1978 to an earnings-related scheme. DHSS leaflet NP32A
deals with retirement pensions for women who are widowed
or divorced.

D.—12

# DIVORCE AT DIFFERENT STAGES

The following fictitious couples illustrate the different financial effects that divorce would bring at various stages of a marriage, depending on commitments, children, jobs and the couples' respective ages. (The reason why the marriage has broken down affects the financial results only in exceptional cases.)

You and your partner will not fit exactly into these examples, but you should be able to identify sufficiently to estimate your own likely financial problems and judge whether it would be possible to divorce on a financially reasonable basis.

If you are seeking the advice of a solicitor, be sure to take with you to the first interview all your financial details and as many as are known of your partner's. It will greatly speed up the case if you and your solicitor have a complete financial picture at the beginning. If this information is made available at too late a stage, costs will have been incurred, even though there was only one likely solution in the first place and the matter could have been settled months previously.

## Stewart and Liza

Stewart, aged 25, a research graduate, marries Liza, a teacher aged 22. She gets a probationary first post and they rent a flat to be near to her school and also convenient for Stewart who goes to his job by train. They save quite hard and pool their earnings in a joint building society account. After two years they buy a small house in their joint names, with the assistance

*example* **201**

of an 85% mortgage. They continue working and generally bring the house up to a good state of repair, sharing the work equally.

STAGE I

| | |
|---|---|
| ages | Stewart 28, Liza 25 |
| number and ages of children | none |
| length of marriage | 3 years |
| matrimonial home | owner-occupied; 2-bed semi |
| equity in home (i.e. if sold, the difference between net sale price and amount owing on mortgage) | £5,000 |
| employment/income | both in work: Stewart earning £8,000 Liza earning £7,000 |

## what happens if they divorce now?

No obvious problem here; there are a number of choices.

### the home

○ The house could be sold and the proceeds split equally between them. This may give each of them enough for a deposit to buy something else. (The costs on one sale and two purchases would be high – solicitors, surveyors, estate agents, stamp duty if applicable, removals.)

○ Stewart could raise the money (perhaps by increasing the mortgage) to buy Liza's half-share (£2,500) for her to put down as a deposit on another, cheaper, property. A problem would be if the value of the house had not risen sufficiently for the building society to lend Stewart a further £2,500, in which case he would have to ask his bank or perhaps his employer for a loan.

○ Liza could find a friend to share with (perhaps a colleague from her school) and they could together 'buy out' Stewart. Building societies have no objection in principle to giving a mortgage to two single people – they are only concerned with ability to repay.

If Stewart is buying out Liza, it will be necessary for Liza to surrender her interest in the property and transfer the legal title, and be released from her personal covenants on the mortgage. And vice versa if Liza buys out Stewart.

**maintenance**
Both are working and independent, so it would not be appropriate for either to be ordered to make maintenance payments to the other, and the couple can be independent of each other in the future. It is important to ensure that all financial claims are made by both of them and are formally dismissed by the court so that they cannot be revived in the future.

Even if Stewart's income were, say, £15,000 compared to Liza's £7,000, he would still be unlikely to be ordered to pay her anything. Only if the wife were not working and had no earning capacity without retraining, might he be required to make maintenance payments, and then they would almost certainly be limited to, say, two years – a 'rehabilitation' period within which she could realistically be expected to establish an earning capacity.

## STAGE II

The couple did not divorce after three years of marriage, but in their fourth year of marriage. They have a baby (John), Stewart is now working for an electronics firm and Liza has decided not to return to teaching for some time.

| | |
|---|---|
| ages | Stewart 29, Liza 26 |
| number and ages of children | one child, under 1 year old |
| length of marriage | 4 years |
| matrimonial home | owner-occupied, 2-bed semi |

*example* **203**

| | |
|---|---|
| equity | £6,000 |
| employment/income | Stewart earning £10,000 shortly to be given a company car; Liza not working, receiving child benefit |

## what happens if they divorce now?

The existence of the child changes the whole picture. The welfare of the child has to be the first concern.

### the home

The child has to have somewhere to live. Usually, the most convenient place is the former matrimonial home and whoever has the child on a day-to-day basis ('care and control') will be able to remain in the home with the baby.

Liza has already given up her job to stay at home and take care of the baby and the court will not expect her to return to work for several years, if she does not wish to do so.

*postponing sale*
It is likely that the court will order that the house should not be sold until the child reaches 17 (or later if there is continued schooling or further education) and the proceeds then split between them. Meanwhile, Stewart will have to house himself elsewhere, without getting any capital out of the home and with a large part of his salary committed to Liza and the child.

The court is likely to transfer more of the equity in the house to Liza because

○ she will be responsible for some 17 years for paying off the mortgage
○ she will be responsible for maintaining the house
○ her future earning (and therefore mortgage) capacity will be substantially less than Stewart's

○ when the house is to be sold, Liza will need accommodation and her financial capacity will probably be limited

○ Stewart will in all probability have acquired a new home and will not have the same need for capital.

Stewart may wish to have a clause in the court order stating that should Liza marry or cohabit, the house should be sold forthwith. The court may be reluctant to agree to this but if these circumstances should arise, Stewart would have the right to apply to the court for a sale.

Alternatively, the house may be transferred to the wife subject to a charge to the husband for about a third of the equity, enforceable on the child attaining the age of majority and thereafter ceasing full-time education, with liberty for him to apply to enforce the charge if the wife cohabits or remarries.

The enforcement of the charge might be deferred for Liza's life or until she voluntarily vacates the home or remarries, particularly if Stewart's job prospects are better than normal.

If Liza wants later to move, in order to buy an alternative house, Stewart's continued interest in the next house would need to be acknowledged. The new house would have to be bought on the same conditions as to sale or enforcement of the charge as before.

A further possibility would be for the house to be transferred to Liza entirely, with her maintenance being reduced from what it would otherwise have been.

### maintenance

There is only one salary, Stewart's, which after deducting national insurance and pension contributions comes to around £9,000. Using the 'one third' formula as a starting point would allocate to Liza an income of £3,000 per annum. (He would have to pay less than that if the child benefit she gets were counted in.) £3,000 is unlikely to be sufficient to pay the mortgage and the bills. Maintenance would be awarded to the baby, perhaps equal to the National Foster Care Association's recommended rates, which would come to about £1,507 p.a.,

*example* 205

and Liza would have that in full. But Stewart would be left with approximately £4,500 which is an insufficient income to live on and raise a moderate mortgage.

So, although stage II is only one year later than stage I, because of the child there is now little choice at all. Stewart and Liza must accept that they are both going to have to struggle financially and that legal arguments will not alter that position.

Liza will need enough money to keep the home going (gas, electricity, rates, water, insurance) and to pay the mortgage, and other outgoings.

Stewart will need enough money to keep up the mainte-nance payments, to pay for his own accommodation (whether renting or buying) and for his day-to-day expenses. Initially, he may also need to buy some household goods, and furniture.

From a tax point of view, the orders should be expressed to make the most of the personal tax allowances. By paying £575 p.a. more to the child (to make his payments £2,082 p.a.) and £2,425 to Liza, she and John would effectively receive more without affecting the amount of total maintenance payments Stewart has to make.

Even so, Liza is not going to have enough for her needs and the baby's and must see how her resources might be increased.

### help from the state
Liza can claim housing benefit from the local authority. The housing benefit scheme is available to owner-occupiers for rates (as well as to tenants for rent and rates).

After divorce, or 13 weeks after separating from her hus-band, the child benefit she gets will be increased by the one-parent benefit (at present £4.70 a week, tax free).

While she is not working, she may be eligible for supplemen-tary benefit. If she goes back to work, she may be eligible for family income supplement which is available to a lone parent who is working for 24 hours a week or more. (Under current government proposals, in April 1988 supplementary benefit is due to be replaced by an income support scheme and family income supplement by a family credit scheme.)

Child benefit and one-parent benefit and any maintenance she receives will be taken into account in full when the DHSS works out her entitlement to supplementary benefit, or the local authority her housing benefit supplement (available to help with housing costs for someone just over the limit for ordinary supplementary benefit).

*maintenance ordered and supplementary benefit*
If there is a likelihood that the proposed maintenance would bring her just above the level which would enable her to claim supplementary benefit, it may be of more practical use to her (and at the same time relieve Stewart of some expenditure) if the maintenance order were for slightly less so that, when assessed by the DHSS, her income would entitle her to supplementary benefit (and its concessions).

## STAGE III

Liza and Stewart continue with their marriage and have a second child (Penny) in their sixth year of marriage. Stewart does well in his job and receives substantial promotion. They move in the following year to a new three-bedroomed detached house bought for £36,500 with a £25,000 20-year endowment mortgage (which means the amount borrowed does not reduce as time goes by).

After a further three years, when the children are aged 6 and 4, Liza returns to part-time teaching. Two years later, they get divorced. They agree to have joint custody of the children with 'care and control' to Liza. She is to remain in the house with the children and Stewart will leave.

| | |
|---|---|
| ages | Stewart 37, Liza 34 |
| number and ages of children | two; aged 8 and 6 |
| length of marriage | 12 years |
| matrimonial home | owner-occupied, 3-bed detached |

*example* 207

equity                              £12,000
employment/income                   both in work: Stewart earning
                                    £17,000 plus company car;
                                    Liza's part-time earnings
                                    £6,000

## what happens if they divorce now?

Still a problem, but not so difficult as at stage II.

**maintenance**

Although there are now children and the mortgage payments
are higher than at stage II, Stewart's increased salary and
Liza's part-time earnings give the couple some freedom of
manoeuvre. Their joint income after deducting national insurance and pension contributions is about £20,000 and one-third
approximately £6,660. Liza's net income is about £5,770 (including child benefit of £7.25 a week per child), so on the
one-third basis, Stewart would have to provide about £900 per
annum for her and something for the children.

If the order for the children were based on the recommended
rate for foster parents, John would get £37.03 per week (£1,926
per annum) and Penny £33.81 per week (£1,758 per annum). In
view of his earnings, this is what the court might well order, as
well as the £900 a year for Liza (so that his payments would
come to a round £4,580 in all).

On the £900, Liza would have to pay tax at 27% (because her
earnings use up her personal tax allowance) but provided
John's and Penny's income is not in excess of their personal tax
allowance of £2,425 p.a. each, no tax will be payable on what
they get. So, from a tax point of view, the orders would
probably be better expressed as a nominal payment for Liza of
5p per annum (provided there is an order, even if it is for only
a nominal amount, an application can be made at any time for
a variation order to increase it if it is necessary) and to increase
the orders for John and Penny. Their orders could be half of the

£4,580 each (£2,290). These (£190 monthly) will count as small maintenance payments, so will be made gross, avoiding cash-flow problems for Liza.

The £4,580 Stewart is ordered to pay to Liza and the children is tax-deductible (in addition to his personal tax allowance of £2,425), so he will have to pay tax on £9,995 (£17,000 *minus* £7,005). Liza, in addition to her personal tax allowance, has the single parent's additional personal allowance (APA) of £1,370.

### the home

There is not sufficient money for them to sell this house and each to buy another. The parents both accept that the children are well settled in the present house. Liza teaches at the school the children attend, which is not far away, so they decide that she shall remain there with the children.

The mortgage will probably have to be changed to a repayment mortgage, in her name (Liza will have enough to make the monthly repayments) or the collateral insurance policy will have to be assigned to her. The present surrender value of the policy will be a factor taken into account in deciding the overall terms of settlement.

### *alternatives*

○ to leave the home in joint names, with a restriction that it is not to be sold until Penny reaches 17 or later if in full-time education (and that if Liza remarries or cohabits, Stewart should have the right to apply for a sale of the house). Stewart will therefore get his share in about 12 years' time, if not sooner. On remarriage or cohabitation, Liza and her new partner could buy out Stewart's share of the house rather than having to move. Meanwhile, he could probably afford to borrow about £20,000 on mortgage, but the mortgagee might not be too happy about this, bearing in mind his continuing liabilities to Liza, and he could get tax relief on only £30,000-worth of both mortgages if he continued to make repayments on the original mortgage. Liza,

*example* 209

on the other hand, may not have enough to re-house herself when the home is finally sold unless she gets more than a half share of the proceeds, on the grounds of carrying the mortgage repayments and upkeep of the house.

○ to transfer the house to Liza but have her claim for periodical payments dismissed (so that she can make no future claims on Stewart) and pay a smaller amount of maintenance to the children. But this would not be a good thing for Stewart if Liza were to remarry (or cohabit) within the next few years, in which case, under the preceding alternative, she would have had to sell the house and share the proceeds with him and be no longer entitled to maintenance.

The advantage of the second alternative for Liza (although she would get less in the way of cash) would be that she could consider moving somewhere smaller and cheaper, to reduce her mortgage and outgoings, and she would not have to give up the house if she remarried.

Stewart, although losing a capital asset, would now be able to borrow on mortgage without too much difficulty. And he can push on in his career knowing that any substantial rises he may receive are his, and not to be drawn on for his ex-wife's maintenance (he may, however, still have to make increases from time to time to the children's maintenance).

## STAGE IV

The couple's marriage survives until their silver wedding and then they split.

| | |
|---|---|
| ages | Stewart 50, Liza 46 |
| numbers and ages of childen | two children aged 21 and 19: John in hotel management away from home, Penny at university |
| length of marriage | 25 years |

| matrimonial home | owner-occupied, 3-bed detached, with a few years of endowment mortgage still to run |
| equity | £41,000 |
| employment/income | both in work: Stewart, a director, earning £30,000, plus company car; Liza, deputy headmistress, earning £11,000. |

## what happens if they divorce now?

Almost as good a position as at stage I.

Stewart and Liza can lead financially independent lives because of their high salaries and the fact that the children are off their hands on a day-to-day basis, although each child will probably need money from time to time and an occasional home during vacations or holidays.

### the home

The house is the three-bedroomed detached one bought new 18 years before. If they both want to sell it, after such a long marriage both would share the proceeds equally, and accordingly Stewart's share and Liza's share is £20,500 plus an equitable split of the contents, plus half the profit on the surrender value of the endowment policy.

If Liza wishes to remain in the home, Stewart's capital in the home would be tied up until she can buy him out, perhaps when the mortgage is discharged in two years' time.

If Stewart wants the house to be sold and Liza does not, the court is likely to agree with him because the house is not now needed for the children.

### maintenance

Stewart may want to make a covenant in favour of Penny while she is a student. Penny's grant entitlement should also be carefully investigated: a maintenance order to her would pre-

*example* **211**

judice the grant because it would count as income in her hands and would reduce her grant £ for £.

Liza might argue that she should receive some maintenance from Stewart, because of his large salary. Whether this is ordered would depend on what is to happen about the house and contents.

The other factor that is relevant here is Liza's loss of pension rights under her husband's employers' scheme. Although she has rights to a retirement pension under her own scheme, she is losing out on a probably substantial lump sum and pension under Stewart's scheme, and at this age such a loss would be significant. So Stewart may be required to compensate her with a lump sum with which she could buy a deferred annuity – again, depending on how they share their interests in the house. The principle of equal division may be subject to adjustment in Liza's favour to compensate for loss of pension rights on the divorce.

# Kevin and Maureen

This couple is typical of many young people for whom, if they divorce having had children, there is no choice at all about money. Going to court is pointless because the result is inevitable.

At 17, Maureen is pregnant when she and Kevin, aged 20, decide to get married. Maureen recently left school and is unemployed. Both sets of parents offer a home to the couple but Maureen wishes to remain with her mother because of the baby. Kevin manages to keep employed on casual work throughout the summer, but is mainly out of work during the winter.

They have a second child in their third year of marriage. Having been on the waiting list for three years and now with two children, they are offered a two-bedroom flat by the council, which they accept. Two years later, they want to divorce. Kevin has had a few months of continuous work with his uncle, but this is likely to come to an end shortly.

| | |
|---|---|
| ages | Kevin 25, Maureen 22 |
| number and ages of children | two, aged 5 and 2 |
| length of marriage | 5 years |
| matrimonial home | council 2-bed flat in their joint names |
| employment/income | Kevin presently employed as a casual labourer – almost certain to be unemployed soon; Maureen caring for children, never had a job |

## what happens if they divorce now?

Almost certainly both will be claiming social security for many years to come.

### the home

Normally the home goes to the person who cares for the children, in this case Maureen. Kevin and Maureen's flat is in their joint names, so the court will order it to be transferred into Maureen's sole name.

The court can order the tenancy, even if it had been in Kevin's name only, to be transferred to Maureen, if she has 'care and control' of the children. She cannot claim the tenancy as of right, neither can she expect to be allocated a property by the local authority once she moves out (unless she is forced to leave because Kevin is being violent and she has to be rehoused under the Housing (Homeless Persons) Act).

Kevin will probably move in with someone else, or return to live with his parents.

### maintenance

As Kevin works only infrequently and his present job is coming to an end, he is unlikely to be able to pay maintenance regularly to Maureen. But the court can make a periodical payments order for a minimum amount, so that this can be varied if the circumstances change. If Kevin is again in work,

*example* **213**

Maureen may feel it worthwhile to try for more maintenance because the court will not accept that Kevin can simply ignore his obligations to his ex-wife and children. She should ask for the increased order to be registered in a magistrates' court, so that she can apply to the DHSS to switch to supplementary benefit if he is not paying. If he is continually or partially unemployed, Maureen would be better off on supplementary benefit which will at least be a regular income.

It is rarely worthwhile pursuing an impoverished ex-husband for maintenance because although the short-term rate of supplementary benefit is low, it is regular and after 12 months the ex-wife automatically transfers to the long-term rate (which is considerably higher); she does not have to register for work while the children are under 16.

While Kevin is unemployed or in irregular work, nothing can alter Maureen's position, at whatever stage they divorce with whatever number of children. She may not be able to get work even later on as she has no particular training, skill or work experience.

Assuming that Maureen does not remarry, she would need to be certain of obtaining significantly more maintenance than a sum which, after tax, would be at least as much as long-term supplementary benefit plus the amounts for two children plus rent and rates from housing benefit, plus the exemptions that come with supplementary benefit.

The future possibilities are

○ Kevin getting well-paid regular work and being able to pay a reasonable amount of maintenance (pretty unlikely)
  or
○ Maureen finding a job and continuing to get some mainte-nance from Kevin (also unlikely)
  or
○ Maureen remarrying or cohabiting (statistically a 1 : 2 chance of this).

In a case like Kevin's and Maureen's, the woman (parent looking after the children) can expect to be on supplementary benefit for many years, caught in the poverty trap.

# ENFORCEMENT OF PAYMENTS

Whatever the court orders, actually receiving maintenance depends on the continuing willingness and ability of the ex-spouse to make the payments.

Should the payer (usually the ex-husband) fall into arrears with maintenance payments, there are several channels for enforcement, none entirely satisfactory. Whichever method is adopted, the sooner steps are taken to enforce the arrears, the better. If arrears are allowed to accumulate, they may well prove impossible to recover. Current case law generally advises courts not to enforce arrears more than a year old.

## enforcing a debt

A defaulting spouse getting away with not paying is part of the wider problem of trying to enforce civil debts in general. Do not be too optimistic about your likelihood of success.

An application for enforcement has to be made to the divorce court that made the order (unless the order has been registered at a magistrates' court). The court will not automatically chase arrears and will only make an order for enforcement if asked to.

The main methods of enforcement are a warrant of execution, an attachment of earnings order, a judgment summons for committal to prison.

### warrant of execution

A warrant of execution is an order issued by the county court for the district where the defaulting payer lives, for the court bailiff to seize sufficient of the person's goods as will on sale by auction discharge the debt shown on the warrant.

Secondhand goods seized and sold at auction rarely produce

much money. It is only worthwhile to get a warrant of execution if the goods are in good condition – but the threat of seizure and sale may produce payment.

To get a warrant issued, you must swear an affidavit showing the amount of the arrears, provide a copy of the order, complete the appropriate county court forms and pay the fee (15p per £ of the amount of the warrant; minimum fee £5, maximum £38); not returnable if there are no saleable goods.

**attachment of earnings order**
Provided that the ex-husband is in regular employment, an attachment of earnings order may be a more effective way of collecting arrears. It requires the employers to deduct regular weekly or monthly amounts from his wages and to send the money to the court who will then pay it to the woman. The amount of deductions can include not only a regular sum off the arrears until they are discharged, but also the ongoing maintenance. (The employers can deduct 50p in addition each time for their pains.) The procedure is no use where the man is unemployed or self-employed.

The application has to be to the divorce county court which made the maintenance order. The appropriate application form (in duplicate) with a copy of the maintenance order, must be supported by an affidavit giving details of the arrears and, if possible, the name of the employers. The court fee for an application is 10p per £ of the amount claimed (minimum fee £5, maximum £40).

A notice of the application is served on the ex-husband, together with a form asking for details of his income and commitments. The court can ask the employers to supply information about the man's earnings over the past few weeks. The applicant should attend the hearing to give up-to-date evidence about the arrears.

*protected earnings*
Any order made will be on the basis that it must not reduce the man's net income below the protected earnings rate. (This is the amount which would be allowed him and his dependants

for supplementary benefit, together with the amount of his rent (or mortgage) and rates and other essential and reasonably long-term commitments, such as other court orders or a hire purchase agreement.) When making an attachment order, therefore, the court may well take the opportunity – after an adjournment if needed for a formal application to be made – to adjust the maintenance order to take account of the realities of the situation as disclosed at the time.

## committal to prison

A judgment summons can be issued for maintenance arrears, if it can be shown that the ex-husband has the means to pay maintenance and has failed to do so; in theory, he can be sent to prison. A judgment summons is a potentially effective means of enforcing payment of arrears where a man has capital or is self-employed and cannot be touched by an attachment of earnings order.

A request for a judgment summons can be made to any county court convenient to the applicant. Legal aid is not available for a judgment summons in the county court but is in the High Court. If the applicant would be eligible, the solicitor should apply to have the case transferred to the High Court.

The woman, or her solicitor, should attend the hearing of the judgment summons, in order to question the ex-husband in an endeavour to prove that he could have paid the maintenance but neglected to do so. If it is proved that he had the means, an order committing him to prison can be made.

Sending him to prison is unlikely to produce the money that the ex-wife needs – although the threat of imprisonment may do so. The order can be suspended if he undertakes to pay regular amounts off the arrears together with current maintenance; it can be reinstated if he fails to keep up the payments.

The court is likely to order the erring ex-husband to pay the fixed costs of the application.

## disappearing ex-husband

If the woman does not know her ex-husband's address, it may be possible to get the DHSS to disclose it to the court because his up-to-date address may be known to them through his national insurance records. A form can be obtained from the court on which the ex-wife should give as much information as she can about his last known address and employer, his date of birth and national insurance number.

The ex-husband's address will not be given to the ex-wife, either by the DHSS or the court.

### enforcement of lump sum or property transfer order

An unpaid lump sum may be enforced either by bankruptcy proceedings (unwise) or by a court order that any property belonging to the person ordered to pay be sold to raise the sum. An order for such a sale (for example, of a house or stocks and shares) can be made when the lump sum is ordered. If not made then, the usual procedure is to apply for a charging order and then for an order for sale of the asset.

If a transfer of property order is not complied with, the registrar at the court can execute the relevant conveyance in place of the person who is refusing to do so. Application has to be made to the court with the relevant documents prepared for the registrar and an affidavit in support.

It is advisable to have a solicitor's help for such enforcement proceedings.


## order registered in magistrates' court

An order made in the divorce court can be registered in a magistrates' court. This means that the magistrates' court staff (unlike in the divorce court) will monitor payments and will summons the payer to appear in court if he or she defaults. The procedure is quicker and simpler.

If a payer is in arrears, the magistrates can order that a disclosure of means be made, and can make one of the following orders

○ attachment of earnings
○ distraint on goods (seizure and sale)
○ committal to prison (for not more than 6 weeks).

# Where to turn

| when | go to | for | provided that | effective |
|---|---|---|---|---|
| marriage breaking up | marriage guidance counsellor | discussion on possibility of reconciliation | prospect of partner coming, too | |
| | conciliation service | mediation to reach agreement on practical matters | prospect of partner coming, too | |
| | solicitor | advice (£5 fixed-fee ½ hour or free at CAB) | | |
| spouse violent to other spouse and/or children | magistrates' court | exclusion or protection order | still married and living together and threat of further violence | from date of order |
| | county court | ouster or non-molestation injunction | | from date of order |

| providing (enough) money | | maintenance and/or lump sum (up to £500) | prove neglect to maintain | order |
|---|---|---|---|---|
| | county court | order for maintenance and/or lump sum | can prove neglect to maintain | from date specified on order |
| | DHSS | supplementary benefit | not in full-time work; resources below set limits | when assessment completed |
| | | or family income supplement | at least one child; earnings below set limits | when assessment completed (lasts for one year) |
| wanting maintenance: during divorce proceedings | divorce county court | maintenance pending suit for wife | divorce petition filed | from date specified on order until decree absolute |
| | | periodical payments for children | | from date specified on order |

219

(continued)

D.—13

220

| when | go to | for | provided that | effective |
|---|---|---|---|---|
| after divorce | divorce county court | periodical payments order | decree nisi pronounced | from decree absolute |
| in agreement about paying maintenance | magistrates' court | agreed maintenance order | still married | from date of order |
| | divorce county court | consent order | divorce petition filed | from date specified on order |
| non-owning spouse wanting to protect right to occupy home | Land Registry (registered property) | registration of a notice | still married to owning spouse | from date of registration until decree absolute (can be extended by order of court) |
| | Land Charges Dept (unregistered property) | registration of a class F land charge | still married to owning spouse | from date of registration until decree absolute (can be extended by order of court) |

| | | | | |
|---|---|---|---|---|
| decision needed re matrimonial home (e.g. who is to live there, how to divide proceeds of sale) | divorce county court | property adjustment order | divorce petition filed; applicant not married again | from decree absolute |
| decision needed re division of family assets | county court | settlement of ownership | still married or less than 3 years since divorce | straightaway |
| | divorce county court | property adjustment/transfer order; lump sum order | divorce petition filed; applicant not married again | from decree absolute |
| ex-spouse failing to make periodical payments as ordered | divorce county court | judgment summons or warrant of execution or attachment of earnings order | that court issued original order | from date of summons, warrant or order |

(continued)

| when | go to | for | provided that | effective |
|---|---|---|---|---|
| ex-spouse failing to make periodical payments as ordered | magistrates' court | enforcement | order registered there and you know where he is | straightaway |
| | DHSS | supplementary benefit | not in full-time work; resources below set limits | when assessment completed |
| | | or family income supplement | at least one child; earnings below set limits | when assessment completed (lasts for one year) |
| wanting change in amount of maintenance being paid | court where original order made or magistrates' court where order registered | variation order | significant change in circumstances, payee not married again | from date specified on order |

# DEALING WITH DEBTS

Divide your debts into priority and non-priority ones.

Priority includes any amount whose non-payment could endanger the possession of your home, such as rent, mortgage payments, second mortgage and any other secured loans; also hire purchase payments on items which you really need (for example, cooker or beds). Other priority debts are fuel bills (non-payment may cause disconnection) or payments into court for maintenance or fines (non-payment of these could result in imprisonment).

**mortgage arrears**
Where the husband has undertaken to continue the mortgage payments, the wife should ask the building society or other lender to keep her informed if he falls behind in the payments, to prevent substantial arrears arising unbeknown to her. Proceedings for possession may be instituted by the building society or other lender against the husband for possession of the house without the wife necessarily knowing about it. If she has registered a charge on the house to protect her right of occupation under the Matrimonial Homes Act, this would not protect where the mortgage is already in existence at the time of registration. But building societies are statutorily required to give notice of any action for possession to a spouse who has registered her right of occupation.

As soon as she is aware of the building society's possession proceedings, the wife should get advice and apply to the court where the hearing is to be held and ask to be joined as a defendant. She could then counter the building society's claim on any ground that would be open to the husband and will have the opportunity to make out a case for saving the home. She is likely to succeed if she can show that it will be possible to pay off the arrears within a reasonable time – that means within one year, or at most two years.

Whenever mortgage payments have fallen into arrears, the wife should speak urgently to the relevant person at the building society and try to arrange some method of discharging the debt. As far as future payments are concerned, if she is on supplementary benefit this should cover the interest part of the mortgage payments.

### rented property
Where the tenancy is in the name of the husband alone, he is liable for paying the rent. If the landlord starts possession proceedings against the husband because of non-payment of the rent, the wife should seek legal advice and apply to be joined as a defendant so that she can use any defence open to the husband under the Rent Acts or Housing Act. This includes the right to apply for the order to be suspended, on condition that she will pay off the arrears of rent by instalments.

The Matrimonial Homes Act gives the wife the right to live in the house or flat up to the date of the decree absolute and provides that payment of the rent, or arrears of rent, by the wife must be accepted by the landlord. If she is to remain there, it is essential that the tenancy be transferred to her, preferably before the decree is made absolute.

Anyone on supplementary benefit is automatically entitled to housing benefit, and someone with income only just above SB level can apply to the local authority for help with housing costs by way of housing benefit supplement. Housing benefit is available, on the basis of income, to tenants both of private and of public landlords.

### *threat of eviction*
Before the worst comes to the worst and you are evicted, get in touch with the local authority (the housing department or the social services department). Under the Housing (Homeless

Persons) Act 1977, the local authority have to take action whenever someone who is homeless or threatened with domestic violence or homelessness approaches them for help in relation to accommodation. This help may be advice only or an offer of temporary accommodation and then rehousing if in priority need – for example, if with children or vulnerable through ill health. A person with whom dependent children are living is considered as having a priority need. Be careful to avoid being treated as 'voluntarily' homeless by choosing to go before you have to.

A booklet *One-parent families: help with housing*, compiled by the National Council for One Parent Families for the Department of the Environment, and available free from OPF, 255 Kentish Town Road, London NW5 2LX, includes specific advice on what to do when a couple split up, covering home owners and tenants.

### rates
If the husband was responsible for payment of the rates while the couple lived together in the home, he will continue to be regarded as liable for the rates up to the decree absolute. But if he has left the home and notified the local authority, the local authority may, in such circumstances, hold the wife liable.

Non-payment of rates is a criminal offence and magistrates can imprison for it.

Failure to pay the rates can result in 'seizure by distress' by the local authority, who have the right to send the bailiff to take away the furniture, unless the spouse who lives there can claim it as being his or her own or can clear the arrears in a single payment or, if the local authority agrees, by instalments.

### gas, electricity and telephone accounts
As soon as your partner leaves, you should transfer future responsibility for these services into your name. You may be asked to settle accounts outstanding from the time when your partner was the customer, but you should refuse to pay any amount due to a previous consumer (whether your spouse or

not). The law in this area is not totally clear and some fuel boards argue that, because you had the benefit of the fuel consumed, you should pay for it. Seek advice if this happens.

If the arrears are yours, straightaway call at the local showroom or contact the accounts department or area manager of the gas or electricity authority or the accounts division of your local telephone area, explain the situation, and ask not to be cut off. (The relevant addresses or telephone numbers are on the bills.) If payment is not made, the undertaking concerned may exercise the right to cut off the supply. If you owe money to a fuel board for items other than fuel (cooker, storage heaters etc.), they cannot disconnect your fuel for non-payment of those amounts.

The gas or electricity authority and British Telecom may be prepared to enter into a fresh agreement with the wife who is left in the home, and take steps against the husband for the unpaid bills. They may be entitled to make the wife pay off the arrears, perhaps by instalments, for the period she has been there on her own before accepting her as the new consumer, or insist on a security payment or deposit. Once the telephone has been cut off, there will be a charge for reconnection.

There is a code of practice governing disconnection of gas and electricity, the effect of which is that supplies should not be cut off if you come to an agreement to pay off by instalments.

A leaflet on *How to get help if you can't pay your bill*, explaining the code of practice, is available from gas showrooms and electricity shops and CABx. If you come up against difficulties about arranging to pay off debts or making future payments, you should contact the area gas consumers' council or electricity consultative council, or get help from the citizens advice bureau or a consumer advice centre.

If you are on supplementary benefit, you can have payment for your arrears deducted from your benefit at a few £s a week – but you will have to pay for current consumption direct.

### hire purchase debts and similar commitments

The person who signed the hire purchase or credit sale agreement is responsible for payment. If the husband continues to pay the instalments, this could be taken into account by the divorce court in assessing the maintenance he has to pay to the wife or, conversely, if the wife pays the instalments.

An order can be obtained from the court transferring to one or other spouse the goods themselves once payments under the hire purchase agreement are completed.

If the husband gets into arrears, the wife has no say in any court proceedings taken by the finance company for return of the goods. However, the company may be prepared to reach an arrangement with her about payment of the money due to them, possibly by smaller instalments, or about terminating the agreement.

The finance company may claim the goods back, but if at least one-third of the price has been paid, a court order must be obtained and the procedure laid down in the Consumer Credit Act must be followed, before possession of the goods can be obtained.

When half the payments due under an HP agreement have been made, the goods can be returned and the hirer (you) owes nothing (except any arrears at that date). Although this means losing all the payments already made, it is useful when you can no longer afford the payments and need to cut your losses or where the goods hired are no longer worth the amount you still have to pay for them – for example, a secondhand car.

Somebody receiving supplementary benefit may get help with HP commitments for essential furniture or household equipment through a weekly addition to the SB payment or perhaps through a single payment towards clearing the debt.

**other debts**
Many other debts are non-priority and will have to wait for payment if you are managing on less money than hitherto. Examples include unpaid county court judgments (you cannot be imprisoned for this type of debt but such a debt may become a priority if bailiffs' action is threatened); arrears on loan agreements, credit sale agreements or credit cards; credit with shops or relatives.

You should work out how much money you have available to pay these debts after allowing for your normal living expenses and paying your priority creditors. Divide up this amount between your non-priority creditors in proportion to the amount you owe them. Write a letter to each of them explaining how much you owe in total and how you have arrived at the offer you are making. Provided some reasonable proposals can be put forward, the creditors may prefer to come to some arrangement rather than rely on their legal rights and take the matter to court.

If you have offered to pay creditors by instalments and they have not accepted, let them sue you. In the meantime, try to keep up the payments you have offered. If it comes to court, the court may order that payment be continued by the instalments unless the creditor can show that you can afford more.

It is a criminal offence to harass a debtor for payment of money: for example, a trader must not threaten to enter the premises to recover the goods. No creditor can enter your house without a court order to take away goods you have bought. Even then, the creditor himself cannot enter: the court order will be enforced by a county court official known as a bailiff (or in a High Court case, a sheriff's officer).

If the bailiff arrives at your door and your spouse, not you, is the debtor, none of your goods should be seized. If the bailiff will not accept that the goods are yours, you should make a written claim to the court and if the creditor does not accept that the goods are yours, the court will issue an 'interpleader' summons. You will have to provide such evidence as you have, by way of receipts, invoices, hire purchase documents, and you may have to attend court to prove your ownership.

If the debt is solely or jointly in your name, the bailiff will be entitled to seize your goods but you may apply to the court to stay execution, usually on the basis that you will pay off the debts by instalments. The county court office will give you the necessary forms to complete.

The procedure in the High Court is more complicated and you may well need legal advice, or advice from a CAB or money advice centre.

**money advice**

Credit and debt are no longer matters to be ashamed of, and much help is available if things get beyond you.

There are financial advice and debt counselling services in some areas, primarily aimed at low-income families. They are provided by voluntary organisations, such as citizens advice bureaux and councils for voluntary service, and by local authority welfare rights departments. Some have an appointment system, some are only for people referred from a CAB or other agency, some are for local residents only. These services are still relatively rare and local, and the picture is always changing.

The Birmingham Settlement Money Advice Centre runs a telephone advice service on mortgage and rent arrears and related debt problems. The 'Housing Debtline' number to ring is 021-359 8501 (Monday and Thursday 10am to 4pm, Tuesday and Wednesday 2 to 7pm). Free information sheets on dealing with debts generally; on arrears of mortgage, rates and water rates; on arrears of rent, rates and water rates; are available from The Birmingham Settlement, 318 Summer Lane, Birmingham B19 3RL.

An increasing number of citizens advice bureaux provide advice and counselling specifically on debts and money problems. They may be able to work out a repayment schedule and help in negotiating with creditors. Generally, the CAB is the place to go to first for help with a money problem; if there is a more appropriate centre locally, the bureau will tell you.

# ADVICE AND HELP

Anyone in difficulties over finance, tax, housing, the children, or rights generally, can go for advice to a **citizens advice bureau.** CAB offices have numerous leaflets and information about local sources of help and services. CABx differ across the country but many can provide you with everything from an impartial listener to representation at social security appeal tribunals or money advice and county court representation. The address of a local citizens advice bureau can be found in the telephone directory.

**The Child Poverty Action Group** (1-5 Bath Street, London EC1V 9PY) publishes *The national welfare benefits handbook* (1987 edition, £4.50) which covers supplementary benefit and other means-tested benefits and *The rights guide to non-means-tested social security benefits* (1987 edition, £4.50) which covers other social security benefits.

**The National Council for One Parent Families** (255 Kentish Town Road, London NW5 2LX, telephone: 01-267 1361) works to help parents who are looking after children on their own. It issues a range of books, reports, pamphlets and information leaflets on problems that a single parent may encounter, including on taxation, housing, social security benefits, divorce and children.

**Gingerbread**, a nationally organised self-help association (headquarters at 35 Wellington Street, London WC2E 7BN, telephone: 01-240 0953), has about 350 local groups providing practical and supportive help and advice for single-parent families. Gingerbread also publishes information leaflets and a quarterly magazine for one parent families. The scottish Gingerbread headquarters is at 39 Hope Street, Glasgow G2 6AE (telephone: 041-248 6840).

**Families Need Fathers** (BM Families, 27 Old Gloucester Street, London WC1N 3XX, telephone: 0689 54343) provides help and support for all non-custodial parents who are having problems over access or custody (not just fathers). FNF has local groups in various parts of the country, and issues a quarterly newsletter (free to members). It has published a booklet *Divorce and your child* (£1) and other booklets on problems encountered by parents apart from their children.

**The National Family Conciliation Council** (34 Milton Road, Swindon, Wiltshire SN1 5JA, telephone: 0793 618486) can give you the address of an affiliated conciliation service in your area or near where you live.

**The National Marriage Guidance Council** has published *The divorce book* (95p from NMGC Bookshop, Herbert Gray College, Little Church Street, Rugby, Warwickshire CV21 3AP), which includes a list of other useful books to read.

**The National Stepfamily Association** (162 Tenison Road, Cambridge CB1 2DP, telephone: 0223 460312) provides advice and support for stepfamilies, and puts members in touch with one another where desired. *The Step-parent's Handbook* (published by Sphere, £2.95) is available from Stepfamily.

Where problems arise over the home – mortgage, occupation of the home, rates, rent and other payments – advice is available from **Shelter** (88 Old Street, London EC1V 9HU, telephone: 01-253 0202, with centres in other towns), and from SHAC (London Housing Aid Centre, 189a Old Brompton Road, London SW5 0AR, telephone: 01-373 7276) dealing with the London boroughs only, or from a local housing aid or advice centre (addresses are listed in the telephone directory). SHAC publications include *The rights guide for home owners* co-published with CPAG (1987 edition, £3.50), *A woman's place* (a guide on rights and relationship breakdown for married women) and *Going it alone* (for single women), £2.50 each.

There are **legal advice centres** in various parts of the country where lawyers working voluntarily give legal advice free (only a limited amount, if any, of further assistance is given). The centres are open only at specified hours. The Legal Action Group publishes a directory of legal advice and law centres available from LAG (242 Pentonville Road, London N1 9UN) or the local CAB or library may have a copy.

The **Department of Health and Social Security** administers most state benefits. The DHSS issues a pamphlet FB2, called *Which benefit?* (available at local social security offices), listing the various ways in which you can get cash help in times of need. It gives current conditions and rates of payment, and refers to other sources of help and information and relevant DHSS leaflets. Leaflet FB27, *Bringing up children?* includes details of benefits available for parents caring for children on their own. There are also leaflets on how to claim various welfare services free, national insurance contribution rates (NI 208) and benefit rates (NI 196), NI guide for divorced women (NI 95), *Your retirement pension if you are divorced* (NP 32A).

There is a DHSS 'freeline' telephone service on 0800 666 555, for general information and guidance on social security benefits, and to ask for relevant leaflets and claim forms.

# GETTING AN UNDEFENDED DIVORCE BY SPECIAL PROCEDURE

| time stage | who acts | action required and documents involved |
|---|---|---|
| 1 — | spouse wanting divorce | may go to solicitor for advice on grounds for divorce and for help with completing petition |
| | | gets appropriate form of petition and, if relevant, statement as to arrangements for children, from divorce county court office or Divorce Registry |
| 2 any time after 1 year from date of marriage | petitioner (spouse wanting divorce) | lodges at court office: completed petition plus copy for spouse (and named co-respondent, if petition based on adultery) certified copy of marriage certificate two copies of completed statement as to arrangements for children, where relevant pays fee of £40 to court office (or completes form to get exemption of fee) |

*continued*

| time stage | who acts | action required and documents involved |
|---|---|---|
| 3 | within a few days of (2) depending on the court's workload | court office | sends to other spouse (respondent) copy of petition, statement as to arrangements for children, notice of proceedings, and acknowledgment of service for completion (in adultery case, all documents except statement re children also sent to co-respondent, if named) |
| 4 | within 8 days of receiving documents in (3) (longer if respondent living outside England or Wales) | respondent (and co-respondent) | must return acknowledgment of service to court (strict time limits apply), plus, if desired, any counter-proposals re arrangements for children |
| 5a | if acknowledgment(s) of service not returned | court office | notifies petitioner and gives information about alternative methods of service |
| b | once acknowledgment(s) of service returned | court office | sends copy of acknowledgment(s) of service to petitioner, plus form of request for directions for trial and form of appropriate affidavit in support of petition, to be completed |

| | | | |
|---|---|---|---|
| 6 | after 8 days from service of petititon if respondent (or co-respondent) has not indicated intention to defend on acknowledgment of service<br><br>**or**<br><br>after 29 days from service of petition if respondent (or co-respondent) indicated intention to defend on acknowledgment of service but has not filed an answer | petitioner | i completes affidavit in support of petition, takes it to a solicitor or court for swearing, plus copy of acknowledgment of service, identifying respondent's signature thereon (and in adultery case, any confession statement from respondent)<br><br>ii completes request for directions for trial (sent at 5b by court office) and takes/sends to court plus<br>    completed affidavit with any relevant supporting documents<br>    copy of any previous court orders relating to the marriage or the children |
| 7 | when request for directions for trial received | registrar | reads and considers the documents |

continued

| time stage | who acts | action required and documents involved |
|---|---|---|
| 8a if all in order | i registrar | enters case in special procedure list<br>certifies entitlement to decree<br>(and to any costs claimed, if appropriate) |
| | ii court office | fixes date for pronouncement of decree by judge and for his consideration of arrangements re children |
| | | sends notification of date(s) to petitioner and respondent |
| b if registrar not satisfied | i registrar<br>ii petitioner<br>iii registrar | requests further evidence or information<br>has to supply required evidence or information to court<br>considers further evidence or information supplied |
| c if registrar then satisfied | i registrar<br>ii court office | grants his certificate as in 8a(i)<br>fixes date for pronouncement of decree by judge and for his consideration of arrangements re children |
| | | sends notification of date(s) to petitioner and respondent |
| d if registrar still not satisfied | i registrar<br>ii court office | removes case from special procedure list<br>informs petitioner and respondent |

| | | | |
|---|---|---|---|
| 9 | on date given in 8a(ii) or 8c(ii) | i judge | pronounces decree nisi (petitioner and respondent need not be present) |
| | | ii court office | sends copy of decree to petitioner and respondent |
| 10 | same day as 9 or on date given in 8a(ii) or 8c(ii) | parent(s) | parent with whom children will live must, the other parent may also, come before judge in chambers to answer questions about arrangements for the children |
| | | judge | considers arrangements for children |
| 11a | if satisfied: same day | judge | certifies satisfaction as to children and, where appropriate, makes orders for custody, care and control, access |
| b | if not satisfied: same day | i judge | may order court welfare officer's report and/or further information from parents and/or refer for conciliation |
| | | ii court office | fixes date for adjourned hearing and notifies parents |
| c | on date fixed in 11b(ii) | parent(s) | attend adjourned hearing before judge with the required additional information |
| | | judge | re-considers arrangements, and, if satisfied, makes appropriate order(s) and certifies satisfaction |

*continued*

238

| time stage | who acts | action required and documents involved |
|---|---|---|
| 12 six weeks and one day after (9) (provided judge has certified satisfaction re children) | petitioner | applies to court (on form available from court office) for decree to be made absolute; pays fee of £10 to court office (or completes form to get exemption of fee) |
| 13 when application in (12) received | court office | checks court records that no reason why decree should not be made absolute |
| | | issues certificate making decree nisi absolute |
| | | sends copy of decree absolute to ex-husband and ex-wife |

**OR**

if petitioner has not applied at stage 12:

| 14a after three months and six weeks since (9) | i respondent | may apply to have decree made absolute, with affidavit in support of application |
| | ii court office | fixes date for application to be heard; returns one copy of application to respondent |

239

| | | | |
|---|---|---|---|
| 14b | by not later than 4 days prior to date fixed for hearing at 14a(ii) | respondent | sends copy of application and notification of date to petitioner |
| c | if over 12 months since decree nisi | i petitioner or respondent | has to apply for leave to make application by lodging written request giving prescribed information re reason for delay; whether parties have lived together since decree nisi; whether wife has borne child since decree nisi |
| | | ii registrar | considers explanation; may require affidavit in support |
| 15a | on date fixed at 14a(ii) | applicant | attends before registrar |
| | | registrar | considers application |
| b | if registrar satisfied | court office | issues certificate making decree nisi absolute |
| | | | sends copy of decree absolute to ex-husband and ex-wife |

# GLOSSARY

**access**
the right granted by the court to the parent with whom the child is not living for the child to visit that parent or stay with him or her for short periods

**acknowledgment of service**
form sent by the court to the respondent (and co-respondent, if any) with the petition, with questions about his or her intentions and wishes in response to the petition; its return to the court establishes service of the petition

**adultery**
sexual intercourse by a husband or wife with someone of the opposite sex at any time before a decree absolute of divorce

**affidavit**
a statement in writing containing a person's evidence, on oath or affirmation. The evidence in the affidavit need not be expressed in any formal way but should be set out in numbered paragraphs in the first person. If the person making the affidavit wishes to refer to any document, this document should be attached ('exhibited') to the affidavit.

**ancillary relief**
general term for the financial or property adjustment orders that the court can be asked to make 'ancillary' to a petition for divorce or judicial separation

**answer**
the defence to a divorce petition, denying the allegations in the

petition or cross-petitioning; strict time limits apply for filing an answer

**application**
a document giving details, in broad terms, of the order sought from the court. All applications within divorce proceedings are started by filing a notice of application. Standard forms are available at divorce court offices; they include a space for the place, date and time of the hearing of the application, to be completed by the court office

**beneficial interest**
the right of a person whether or not having legal ownership of a property to use or occupy it and to have a share in the proceeds if it is sold

**Calderbank letter**
where a husband knows he will be ordered to make payment if case goes to hearing, his solicitor writes letter making an offer of settlement and costs; if wife rejects offer and at hearing is awarded less, wife risks having to pay husband's costs incurred after date of offer as well as her own

**care and control**
the responsibility for looking after and making everyday decisions about a child and providing the child's main home base

**certificate of deduction of income tax (form R. 185)**
has to be supplied to the inspector of taxes by the recipient of maintenance paid net of tax; the payer completes a certificate at regular intervals and sends it to the recipient

**in chambers**
when the judge or registrar considers an application in private rather than in open court; the proceedings tend to be less formal than normal court hearings

**charge (on property)**
security entitling the holder of the charge to be paid out of the proceeds of sale when the property is eventually sold

**chattels**
personal possessions – worldly goods (in the sense of 'goods and chattels'), particularly house contents, car, etc.

**child of the family**
any child of both the parties and any child who has at any time been treated by both the parties as if a child of their own (but not foster-children); has to be listed in the petition irrespective of age

**clean break**
a 'once and for all' order that deals with all financial issues between spouses and is not capable of subsequent variation even if circumstances change

**common fund**
the highest level of costs awarded (generally when legally aided)

**conciliation**
a process of non-partisan mediation to help a couple reach agreement on issues such as the arrangements for children, including custody and access disputes

**consent order**
order made by a court in terms agreed by both parties

**co-respondent**
the person with whom the respondent is alleged to have committed adultery

**counsel**
barrister

**cross-decrees**
when a petitioner is granted a decree on the basis of the petition and the respondent on the basis of the answer

**cross-petition**
when the respondent puts forward in the answer different reasons for the breakdown of the marriage from the petitioner's, and seeks a divorce on those facts

**custody**
the right granted by a court for one parent (or both) to make major decisions for a child, such as education and upbringing, change of religion (subject to the non-custodial parent's right to ask the court to review any such decision)

**decree absolute**
the order dissolving the marriage

**decree nisi**
document issued once the court is satisfied that the grounds for divorce are established, allowing the petitioner to apply to have the decree made absolute after a further six weeks

**directions for trial**
the stage of divorce proceedings when the registrar considers the petition and affidavit in support and requests further information if required before giving his certificate for a decree nisi to be pronounced by the judge

**disclosure**
full information about all matters relevant to any financial application; each spouse has a duty to give full and frank disclosure

**discovery**
procedure by which each party supplies to the other a list of documents relevant to an application and permits the other to inspect them

**divorce court**
any county court designated by the Lord Chancellor as a court
where divorce proceedings can be heard; also the Divorce
Registry in London

**domicile**
legal concept, not necessarily related to residence: domicile of
origin is normally determined by the place where a person was
born and is retained unless a new domicile – a domicile of
choice – is adopted by a conscious decision to take up permanent residence in, and actually moving to, another country

**endowment mortgage**
where a life insurance policy is charged to the building society
or other mortgagee as collateral security, the borrower pays
the premiums to the insurance company and interest only to
the building society; if the borrower dies or when the policy
matures at the end of the mortgage term, it provides at least the
amount needed to pay off the loan in full

**equity (of a house)**
the right to all or a share of the proceeds of sale (the net value
after mortgage debts are discharged and expenses of sale met)

**exhibit**
document referred to in, sworn with, and attached to an
affidavit; usually identified by initials and number

**filing**
leaving documents – petition and accompanying documents,
affidavits, notices of application – with the court office for
sealing, and subsequent service

**green form**
popular term for scheme under which a limited amount of
legal advice and assistance is given free or against assessed
contribution

**injunction**
order by the court telling someone what he or she must or must not do; the penalty for disobedience can be imprisonment

**legal aid**
government-funded scheme administered by the Law Society based on financial eligibility and merits of case. What you pay towards your solicitor's bill is

o any contribution you are assessed to pay out of your disposable income and/or capital
o payment out of any money or property gained or preserved which is subject to the statutory charge.

Your being legally aided does not preclude your opponent being ordered to pay some or all of your costs. If costs are awarded against you, you personally have to pay (the legal aid fund will not) but your liability for your opponent's solicitor's bill will be limited to what the court considers reasonable for you to pay.

**liable relative proceedings**
proceedings taken against person legally responsible for maintaining wife or husband and/or children who has failed to do so

**minutes of order**
draft terms of agreement placed before the court with a request that a consent order be made in those terms

**mortgagee**
the building society, bank or other corporate lender or individual lending money on the security of a house or flat

**mortgagor**
the person who borrows money on mortgage usually to enable him or her to buy a house or flat

**nominal order**
when recipient is entitled to maintenance but at the time of the order payment cannot be made or is not needed, an order for a nominal amount of maintenance (for example, 5p a year) is made so that if circumstances change, there is an order on the court's file which can be reviewed and varied

**non-molestation**
order to prohibit one person from assaulting, harassing or interfering with another

**notice of application**
form on which applications to the court are made, beginning with the words 'Take notice that . . .' and containing full details of what is applied for

**ouster**
order excluding one spouse from the matrimonial home

**party-and-party costs**
the proportion of the other party's solicitor's bill which has to be met by the person who is ordered to pay costs

**petitioner**
the person who initiates divorce proceedings by filing the petition

**postal divorce**
colloquial term for divorce by special procedure

**prayer**
formal request in the petition, or answer, for the court orders which the petitioner or respondent seeks: for example, dissolution of the marriage, custody, costs, ancillary relief

**questionnaire**
list of questions delivered by one spouse to the other requiring further information and/or documentation about finances, in accordance with that person's duty of disclosure; also referred to as 'request under rule 77(4)' – the rule of court permitting such a questionnaire

**quickie divorce**
colloquial term for divorce by special procedure in Scotland

**recommendation**
barrister's statement when dispute referred to Family Law Bar Association's adjudication scheme

**registrar**
judicial officer appointed by the Lord Chancellor; responsible for dealing with most of the applications to a divorce court

**relevant child**
child of the family under 16 years of age at the date of the decree or between 16 and 18 years of age receiving instruction at an educational establishment or undergoing training for a trade, profession or vocation (or up to any age, if disabled); the court has to express satisfaction about the arrangements for such a child before decree nisi

**reply**
document filed by the petitioner in response to an answer and/or a cross-petition from the respondent, containing the petitioner's defence

**reserved costs**
when decision on amount of costs to be awarded is deferred until later hearing

**respondent**
the spouse who is not the petitioner

**rule 76A**
the rule of court relating to the statement of information which
has to be supplied to the divorce court for a consent order to be
made

**sealing by the court**
the court's stamping of a document when it is filed at the court
office or of an order or decree when it is issued

**section 41 appointment**
or 'children's appointment' – short hearing before a judge for
certificate of satisfaction in respect of arrangements for any
relevant children before decree nisi can be pronounced

**secured provision**
when some income-producing asset of the payer is put under
the control of trustees and, if necessary, the income diverted to
the payee to provide the maintenance ordered

**service**
the method by which the petition, notices of application,
orders and decrees are supplied to the parties concerned;
certain documents need to be served personally, others are
served through the post, some by or on behalf of the person
issuing them and some by the court

**small maintenance payments**
when a maintenance order is for weekly or monthly payments
of not more than £48 a week or £208 a month to a spouse or to
a child, or to a spouse for a child of not more than £25 a week
or £108 a month, the payments are made in full without
deduction of tax by the payer

**solicitor-and-own-client costs**
proportion of solicitor's bill to be paid under an order for costs
on this basis

**special procedure**
in an undefended divorce, the decree can be issued without either petitioner or respondent having to appear (or be represented) at the court: the facts submitted by the petitioner in the petition and verified on affidavit are considered by the registrar at the divorce court. When he is satisfied that the facts in the petition are proved and that the ground for a divorce exists, he issues a certificate to that effect and fixes a date for the formal pronouncement of the decree nisi by the judge. A copy of the decree is sent through the post to both husband and wife by the court office.

**special procedure affidavit**
the affidavit sworn in support of the petition and filed with a request for decree nisi

**spouse**
either one of a married couple

**statement of arrangements**
form which has to be filed with petition if there are relevant children, setting out arrangements proposed for them in the future

**statutory charge**
the amount payable by legally aided person out of any property or cash that was in issue in the proceedings and was recovered or preserved, where contributions to legal aid fund not sufficient to meet cost of the case (in matrimonial proceedings, £2,500 is exempt)

**summons**
demand issued by a court for a person against whom a claim or complaint has been made to appear at the court at a specified time

**undefended divorce**
where the dissolution of the marriage and how it is to be
achieved is not disputed (even if there is dispute about ancillary matters such as custody of children or finances)

**undertaking**
promise to the court to do or not do something which is outside
the court's powers to order but is incorporated within a court
order so that it is enforceable; the court has no power to vary an
undertaking

**without prejudice**
phrase used to prevent communications in negotiation process
being made known to the court if those negotiations fail to
produce agreement

# INDEX